three-dimensional
textiles with coils, loops
knots and nets

three-dimensional textiles

with coils, loops knots and nets

Ruth Lee

BATSFORD

Dedication

For Barbara Santos-Shaw-Chang: a very special thank you to a wonderfully inspiring tutor at Liverpool College of Art, for everything you taught me, your encouragement and, above all, those much-needed challenges to go one step further than I ever thought was possible.

First published in the United Kingdom in 2010 by
Batsford
10 Southcombe Street
London W14 0RA

An imprint of Anova Books Company Ltd

ISBN-13: 9781906388645

A CIP catalogue record for this book is available from the British Library.

15 14 13 12 11 10
10 9 8 7 6 5 4 3 2 1

Reproduction by Rival Colour Ltd, UK
Printed by Craft Print International Ltd, Singapore

This book can be ordered direct from the publisher at the website: www.anovabooks.com, or try your local bookshop.

Distributed in the United States and Canada
by Sterling Publishing Co.,
387 Park Avenue South, New York, NY 10016, USA

This twined form has been hand-dyed with direct dyes. It has been constructed using viscose tubular ribbon filled with sisal string, twined with rayon seam binding tape.

Contents

Introduction

This book explores methods of creating innovative and experimental textile-based surfaces and forms using traditional off-loom construction techniques that do not rely on large-scale textile machinery for production. Written for contemporary textile makers and fibre artists, the techniques described here include looping, twining, knotting, netting, wrapping, binding and coiling.

Traditionally, these non-loom-woven techniques are generally associated with basketry and similar crafts, such as making mats, fishermen's nets, ceremonial artefacts, costumes, domestic utensils and tribal dwellings. In the context of this book these techniques are interpreted using relatively soft fibres, although sometimes in combination with harder materials and a variety of surface treatments.

Each chapter takes the reader through the basics of the construction process with clear, 'how-to' illustrations. These are followed by suggestions for many alternative interpretations for potential gallery pieces or applied textile artworks.

Experimental form, knotted in the round. The cordage was made on a sewing machine using reclaimed fabrics and yarns (see page 17).

Once the basic moves of a particular technique become second nature, the reader is encouraged to take ownership of that technique and progress towards making work that uses the technique to interpret a particular idea or source of reference. This is not dissimilar to making a drawing from marks and lines, only in this case working with fibres and textiles.

It is not intended that the reader should see each working method as a stand-alone technique, but as part of the bigger picture. The methods are a means to an end, and can be cross-referenced and combined to achieve a particular vision that is far removed from their original purpose and function.

It would plainly be an impossible task in one volume to cover every facet of such a diverse range of techniques, each one in great depth. The focus therefore of each chapter is on a particular aspect (or aspects) of any given working method. For example, the chapter on knotting (chapter 3) explores in some depth the distinctive features of a small selection of knots, and looks at how they can be manipulated to create relief surfaces and three-dimensional forms in a range of materials and sizes for assorted purposes.

Readers of all skill levels are encouraged to develop their tactile sensitivity through hands-on experimental making, alongside a thoughtful approach to the many formal elements involved in creating textile art (for example colour, shape, texture, form, rhythm, pattern, composition and underlying structure).

The physical properties and individual characteristics of a wide range of linear materials are discussed and sampled throughout the book. For the textile artist it is also about discovering how the tactile qualities of certain materials might speak to them and, in turn, communicate something of the artist's intent to a wider audience.

Of equal importance is the inter-relationship between materials, technique and working methods, and how these choices affect the making process in the construction of surfaces and forms to ensure that they have both structural integrity and visual appeal.

A thorough understanding and working knowledge of materials and technique, sound manual dexterity and a skilful use of technical expertise are prerequisites for good practice within the fibre arts. This body of knowledge, built up over time, underpins the ability of the working textile artist to address design issues and artistic concepts with the confidence to break rules and create innovative works.

Without the confidence to break rules, textile artwork would simply be a technical exercise, lacking in innovation and depth. Equally, without the body of knowledge, built up over time, the scope of the designer-maker or textile artist would be limited to a narrow horizon.

The essentials

In this first chapter, the essential tools and equipment for constructing three-dimensional textiles are discussed. There are also examples of very useful tools for more specialist purposes. All of the techniques covered in the book can be worked with small-scale tools and portable equipment, without the need for expensive machinery. For example, a hand-held cord winder can be used for plying yarns and a domestic sewing machine can be used to create handmade cordage from reclaimed fabrics.

A little history

It is worth bearing in mind that in primitive societies, traditional techniques relied entirely on what was available in the local environment for tools and raw materials. This led to an intimate knowledge of just what the natural environment could offer in the way of fibres, their properties and potential uses. This constitutes a considerable body of knowledge that should never be overlooked by the contemporary textile artist.

For instance, in traditional cultures, naturally occurring gums and resins were used to make vessels watertight and colours were sourced from plant-based dyestuffs. Mineral, animal and vegetable materials were used in all aspects of traditional basket making, and included feathers, stones and shells for decoration. Depending upon what was available locally, string and sewing materials would be made from animal fibres and sinews, cordage from plant fibres, while various roots, stems and bark were used for constructing domestic and ceremonial artefacts.

Traditional basket makers might have used their knees to support and tension their work, or as a way of creating dome shapes, before evolving moulds and plugs that conformed to the interior surface of the basket. Similarly, the textile artist today can make use of a wide range of three-dimensional shapes in modern materials to assist in the construction of their work; a technique that is particularly useful in knotting, twining and coiling in three dimensions.

Tools and equipment

Formers or temporary moulds

For your formers choose surfaces that can be pinned into, or that tape will stick to: for example, cardboard cones and tubes, florists foam blocks (not oasis, which is too crumbly), foam water-pipe insulation material or polystyrene balls. If you are taking a DIY approach, consider using plant pots and other plastic shapes covered with bubble wrap, quilt-makers wadding or simply wrapped with masking tape.

Useful for constructing knotted and twined forms, moulds can be customized with further padding to create irregular shapes, by taping layers of bubble wrap or wadding over selected areas. Take care when creating padded-out sections that the knotted or twined form can still be removed easily from the mould; in particular, beware of creating undercuts in the newly shaped mould.

If you are using a cone as a former as shown below, work in progress can be relocated and moved higher up towards the narrow end, creating irregularities in the shape by drawing in the structure as you knot or twine closely to the former. To increase the shape dramatically, simply unpin the work from a wide mould and replace it onto a narrower shape. You could even use both ends of a cone former.

Other working methods for constructing three-dimensional forms include padding out the work in progress with scrunched-up tissue paper or bubble wrap, instead of using a mould. Another method is to work in the round over a mould to establish the shape, and then move on to working freehand.

For piecing individual units of work together over a curved surface, try using a soft, padded dress form, hat block or shoe form, or a sleeve-head pressing block, which can be pinned into.

Couronne or ring stick

The couronne or ring stick is a temporary former, made of wood with stepped graduations. It is traditionally used in Hedebo embroidery (a Danish type of openwork embroidery) for making small, detached rings from thread, worked in buttonhole stitch, which are then incorporated in openwork designs. It is useful for making detached coils for wrapping or incorporating into coiled pieces (see chapters 4 and 5).

Knotting in the round using a cardboard cone as a temporary former.

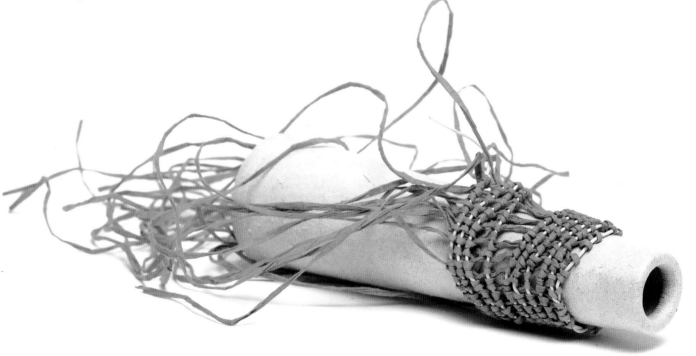

Skein winder

A skein winder or umbrella swift (or your own DIY version) is essential for winding yarns into skeins and hanks for dyeing.

A simple DIY skein winder can be made using a length of wood with two wooden or metal posts (such as copper tubing) set at opposite ends, between which you can wind the yarn. Secure with a G-clamp attached to the tabletop.

Cord winder or rope maker

A cord winder or rope maker is essential for twisting multiple ends of yarn into two-, three- and four-ply cordage. The principle of cord making involves putting a clockwise twist into individual plies, and then twisting them together anticlockwise while under tension so that they twist together into one cord.

Low-cost versions include purpose-made single-hook twisters, where each ply is twisted clockwise separately, then parked on hooks placed alongside the drill, while still attached to the outer point to keep a constant tension. When all four plies have been twisted, they are all placed onto the twister hook and twisted together counter-clockwise. A hand drill, or an electric drill that allows you to wind the wheel in both directions, can be modified for this task.

To make two-, three- or four-ply cordage where all cords are twisted at the same time, various pieces of equipment are available, including lightweight battery-operated devices, which are useful for small projects, or simple wooden hand twisters supplied with alligator clips to hold the separate plies. Hooks or similar devices are needed to hold the plies under tension while being laid out prior to twisting, as maintaining a constant tension is vital.

More sophisticated hand-operated cord makers include the Anna Crutchley cord twister (see opposite) and the Apollo cord winder. Both are hand-operated cord makers. The former comes with its own parking stand for the winder, and a set of four mounted cup-hooks that are clamped to a table, so that a single operator can lay the plies under a constant tension between the two. The Bradshaw cord winder comprises a cord-making cylinder head that attaches to an electric drill.

For an alternative, have a look at rope-making machines, which can be purchased or made from plans.

Sewing and knitting machines

A sewing or knitting machine is a useful but not essential tool. Use a sewing machine to stitch together fabric tubes for filling. To make machine-stitched cordage, set the machine to sew various widths of zigzag stitching over bundles of yarn, or thin strips of fabric. A custom-made cording foot is available for some makes of sewing machine (such as Bernina, for example).

Use a knitting machine to knit lengths of knitting for felting and cutting into strips. A basic, single-bed machine with a slip-stitch setting is all that is needed to make mock cords (see page 20).

The Fasturn™ system

Turned and filled fabric and tubular knitting can be made easily and quickly with a series of gadgets from www.fasturn.net. Tubular chainette yarns in cotton and viscose fibres (from Texere Yarns) have been turned and filled with wire and sisal string, using some of the narrow diameter tubes from the Fasturn™ system to make highly successful weavers and warps for several of the projects in this book.

In the Fasturn™ system, copper or plastic tubes in different diameters, with plastic collars, are used in conjunction with a wire hook to turn strips stitched from lengths of fabric, and at the same time insert a filler cord or wire.

The fabric tube is hooked up in such a way that it can be pulled through the metal tube and turned to the right side in one operation, along with any filler (such as cord, wadding and cable).

The fabric tube, with the wrong side facing outwards, is pulled over the end of a suitably sized metal tube, and pushed down as far as the plastic collar. The length of the turned and stuffed tube will depend on how much fabric can be accommodated on the tube. Longer lengths will need to be joined (see also pages 18–20).

Japanese screw punch/book drill

The screw punch or book drill is a truly versatile and robust tool, primarily intended for bookbinding. It has seven different and interchangeable bits (sizes 1mm to 5mm) for punching holes into various surfaces, including Lutradur, Tyvek and Tissutex papers (see chapter 8). Holes can also be punched in thin leather and stiffened fabric. The Japanese screw punch has a wooden handle and brass shaft, and uses downward pressure to spin the drill bit to punch out holes. Holes can be punched anywhere on a surface, and it is not limited in distance from the edge.

The Anna Crutchley system comes with a cord twister (A) and stand (C) plus four mounted cup hooks (D) and a clamp (B) to attach the hooks to a work surface.

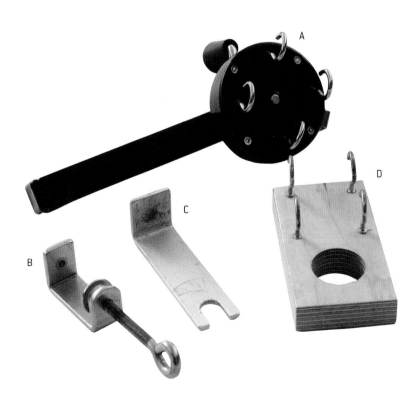

The tool is best used with a self-heal cutting mat, as the drill bits may damage the working surface. Lightweight materials such as Lutradur may need to be taped down onto the mat, particularly if working through multiple layers, to stop the bottom layer twisting. If you are punching a single, lightweight surface you will find it easier if a few sheets of newspaper are sandwiched between it and the cutting mat.

Screw block

A screw block is used in basket making to hold uprights secure. It can also be utilized for three-dimensional construction techniques, particularly for twining techniques.

A DIY version can easily be made from two lengths of wood joined at each end by long coach bolts with nuts, which can be used to separate and join the lengths of wood like vice-jaws.

Knotting equipment

When you are knotting you will need a suitable surface to work on. If you are simply making knotted chains, then the header cord can be strung between two nails hammered into a piece of wood measuring 3.5 x 2 x 60cm (1½ x ¾ x 24in), which can then be clamped easily to a tabletop.

Chains of knots made using paper cord and yarn. Yarns of various thicknesses are added to and removed from the core and knotting yarns.

Alternatively, use any kind of round profile bar, such as wooden dowels, knitting needles or metal or plastic rods, which can be attached to a knotting board with either T- or U-shaped pins, or taped to a table with duct tape. For flat circular knotting, use a wooden ring as a starting point. Another alternative working surface, dating from the Victorian period, is a weighted pillow filled with sand.

Long cords can be wound around cardboard bobbins or similar to stop them tangling. Other methods include tying the working cords into butterfly bundles secured with an elastic band, chaining the cords together and shortening the working cords by tying a temporary double half-hitch knot (see page 33), which can be slid along the cord to let out more length as needed.

Netting needles

Netting needles are not always easy to source, but they can be found on auction sites or from marine suppliers. They act in the same way as a shuttle, and come in a variety of sizes and materials (wood, metal and plastic). Some netting shuttles form a double-ended needle, while other types can be used from one end only. They are especially useful for knotless netting projects (see chapter 7): a considerable length of string can be wound onto them, eliminating the need for numerous joins. DIY versions can be made from plywood or similar.

Other useful tools

- Weights from balance scales to hold work in position when working flat on the table. Also useful are clothes pegs, small plastic clamps, electrical PVC tape and masking tape.
- Rotary cutter and self-heal cutting mat for cutting fabric into strips and circles.
- Cork or foam board to pin into, to secure work in progress for knotting. Cup hooks can be screwed into the top of the board to support header cords, or wooden dowel.
- Sewing notions, such as bodkins and large-eyed tapestry needles, curved upholstery needles, various pins, long quilt-makers' pins, T-pins, notice-board pins and sewing awl.
- Cutting tools, such as sharp scissors, craft knives, pliers, wire-cutters and rotary cutters.
- Knitting and crochet equipment. A range of knitting needles in small, medium and large sizes up to at least 25mm (1in). Double-pointed needles are useful for making tubes in rounds, as are various sizes of spools. Crochet hooks in a range of sizes are always handy.
- Dyeing equipment. For cold-water dyeing with Procion MX reactive dyes, use a plastic bowl or bucket, and a wooden or plastic spoon or stick to stir with. For hot-water dyeing with acid dyestuffs, disperse dyes and direct dyes, use a stainless-steel pan, avoiding iron, copper or aluminium containers as these can affect the shades of the dyes. An old-fashioned baby Burco wash boiler with a covered element is ideal if you can track one down. Use a wooden, plastic or stainless steel stirring stick.

Health and safety issues relating to the use of dyestuffs are covered in some depth on pages 126–127 and should be given careful attention.

Transformations

This chapter is all about transforming fibres and textile-related materials through dyeing, colouring and various surface treatments.

Handmade cordage

Throughout the book there is an emphasis on using handmade cordage rather than simply relying on off-the-shelf yarns in their bought-in state.

Techniques for making cords are described in this chapter, and include working on a domestic sewing machine using the zigzag or cording presser foot, or using a cord twister to make colourful and decorative two-, three- and four-ply cords. Filled, ruched and gathered cordage is made easily and quickly with the Fasturn™ system (see page 11).

Fibres used in this collection include 100 per cent wool, wool and linen mix and slub cotton. The machine-stitched cordage is made from recycled silk scarves, embroidery thread and 0.1mm craft wire.

Over-dyeing coloured yarn you already have in your stash, or dyeing undyed yarns from first principles, are two ways of adding that extra something to textile artwork, and should be encouraged for an individual look.

Many of the samples in this book were piece-dyed once they had been made (see the samples on pages 44, 116–117 and 122 for example). Some of the cordage was dyed to a particular colour story and then used to construct the work (see, for example, the darker moody colours used in chapter 6).

All the pieces in this 'Rag Pot' collection demonstrates coiling techniques using hand-dyed, handmade cordage.

Making weavers and warps from scratch

Twisting and plying yarns and fibres

Plying together existing colours in a particular colour story is a good way of extending the creative possibilities of already-dyed, off-the-shelf yarns. Many of the examples shown in chapter 4 were made in this way.

A number of different devices for making plied cordage have already been described in chapter 1 (see page 10). These are used for twisting multiple ends of yarn into two-, three- and four-ply cordage. The technique consists of putting a clockwise twist into individual plies, then twisting them together anticlockwise while under tension.

A cord twister device is a more sophisticated way of making cordage compared to the time-honoured method of tying a bundle of yarns around a stationary point, such as the door handle, twisting by hand in one direction, then allowing them to twist around themselves at the midpoint.

Between two and four separate elements can be twisted together using, for example, the Anna Crutchley cord twister (as shown on page 11).

Each of the four elements can consist of multiple ends in varying textures, colours and thickness. However, it should be noted that yarns twist up at different rates, which could cause problems if used in the same piece of finished cordage. This is very noticeable when putting the twist into individual bundles of yarns, as the problem ones will twist together into much shorter, or longer, lengths than the remaining elements.

There are always creative possibilities with such perceived mistakes, but it is wise to understand why this is happening so that the effect can be controlled.

Handmade cordage using off-the-shelf colours plied together using a cord twister.

Note also that commercial yarns are spun with a Z-twist or an S-twist, so there is the possibility that they will untwist when using this method of working.

Machine-stitched cordage

In contrast to the relative softness and fluidity of the plied cords outlined opposite, this technique is suitable for making firmer cordage, suitable for weavers and weft in twining, and three-dimensional knotting techniques, coiling and wrapping in particular.

I make machine-stitched cordage on my Bernina 1015 sewing machine using the cording foot (number 21), various combinations of yarns being fed through the hole in the presser foot and over-stitched using differing widths of zigzag stitch. I use fine wire (0.1mm) in the bobbin, with a machine embroidery thread chosen for the top thread (see also the samples on page 40).

Machine-stitched cordage in an experimental two-part form that combines coiling, wrapping and twining techniques.

Choose related thread and yarn colours, perhaps from the same quadrant of the colour wheel, for example green-blues, greens and yellow-greens; or alternatively opposite colours, for example blues and oranges. If you are making a series of cords to be used in the same project, consider over-stitching all the bundles of yarns in the same threads to tie the various colours together.

The same principle can be applied to working with thin strips of patterned fabrics. Pick out a colour from the fabric for the over-stitching, or run a thin yarn alongside all the different fabric strips. Alternatively, unify the work by over-dyeing the lengths of cordage in the same dye bath.

Over-stitching very thin strips of fabric, for example strips from old silk scarves in multicoloured patterns, can work well and give some surprising results and juxtapositions of colour (see samples on pages 6 and 34, for example).

In many of the examples in this book, strips of fabric were torn lengthways down the long edges of an old scarf or similar, each approximately 1.5cm (½in) wide. The raw edges of the torn strips will roll around themselves as the fabric is threaded through the presser foot. To help the process along, gently twist the fabric strip from time to time, being sure to observe safety precautions with the sewing machine, keeping hands well away from moving parts and the needle plate.

To make a continuous length of cordage, taper the end of the strip being stitched, and the beginning of the new strip, twisting both strips loosely together to conceal the joins. A second line of stitching in a different colour or type of thread can be worked over the first row of stitches.

There are limitations to this technique, notably the amount (bulk) of threads or fabric that can be inserted into the presser foot at any one time. To create bulkier cords, try plying or twisting these thin ends together, using a cord twister or similar, or make them into a crochet or finger-knitted chain.

Fabric strips and tubes

Hand-dyed warps can be constructed from lengths of handmade cordage, which have an outer sleeve of 100 per cent tubular stockinet filled with single-core electrical cable (see samples on pages 77, 79 and 81 for example).

To make a similar sample, using an appropriately sized Fasturn™ tube, pull lengths of tubular-knitted chainette over the top of the cylinder until it is full. You can squash the chainette down to get the maximum length of cord. Do not break off the chainette, as you will be incorporating the other end, along with the wire as part of the filler.

Fold the end of the chainette over the cylinder opening, and hold firmly in place with one hand. With your other hand, insert the Fasturn™ wire up the tube from the bottom, piercing the chainette, twisting the wire to the right until the little hook on the end of the wire is through the chainette. Hold onto the handle of the hook and, without twisting it, pull about 2cm (¾in) of the chainette down into the tube.

Keeping hold of the handle, insert the connecting cable into the tube alongside the chainette, making sure it is not caught in the hook, and pull gently on the wire so that the chainette is turned outside-in with the wire. At the same time, the extra end of chainette, plus the wire, is pulled into the tube. Cut the filler threads and wire, and remove from the Fasturn™ tube.

This type of cordage can be over-stitched with machine-sewn zigzag stitches to make it more rigid, particularly if a very fine craft wire is used in the bobbin. A note of caution: if you are using cable or wire as a filler, make sure that the width of the sewing stitch clears the cable.

Ruched, filled and turned fabric tubes

A series of ruched, filled and turned cords can be constructed from soft, tubular chainette yarn (Texere 100 per cent cotton ribbon) over a core of the same, plus one strand of plastic-covered wire as shown in the sample below (see also the samples on pages 107, 109 and 112).

Make the cord as described above. To ruche the cord, tie a knot at one end and push the chainette down the wire, making some areas more ruched than others. Cut off the excess wire, making sure that you secure the end of the cord with a knot. You can also ruche as you turn, to save on wastage with the wire core. Simply pull the wire back up through the opening of the Fasturn™ tube, so that the chainette ruches as you turn.

Filled, turned and ruched cords in hollow chainette cotton ribbon. The filler used for this sample is electrical cable.

Knitted and turned tubes

Knit long lengths of mock-tubular cords in industrial weight lambswool, at the loosest possible tension. Use a single-bed knitting machine on a slip-stitch setting, changing colour at regular intervals. As this is a very loose tension, the stitches will be big and open in relation to the recommended gauge of the yarn. To emphasize the gaps, you could also knit on every other needle.

Here is how to do it: cast on five stitches (for example) and set the carriage to knit in one direction, and slip (i.e. the stitches will not knit) in the opposite direction. Knit a length twice as long as required. Process the knitted length on the Fasturn™ tube as described on pages 18–19. Half of the knitting will be the outer covering, while the other half forms the filler.

The effect is the same as hand-knitting with a very thin yarn on big knitting needles. A great technique for doing this is to use jumbo-sized double-pointed needles (from Addi) and knit in one direction only. At the end of each row, do not turn the work; instead push the knitting back to the end of the needle where you started knitting. Knit another row. Repeat this sequence as many times as required to knit an i-cord.

Recycle, reinvent and reuse resources

An environmentally friendly use of resources is to be encouraged in your sampling and making wherever possible. Look also for commercial manufacturers of yarns and fibres that demonstrate responsibility for environmental concerns.

The undyed yarns used throughout the book are available from Texere Yarns (see Suppliers, page 124) and include various weights of recycled cotton cord in ecru and white, which are ideal for wrapping and coiling core fibres.

Biodegradable ribbons are produced by the Lawrence Schiff Silk Mills (see Suppliers, page 124). Look for the earth-friendly eco twist ribbon, which is 100 per cent compostable paper (www.custompaper.com).

Before buying new supplies, consider ways of using creatively the stash of materials all textile artists accumulate over time, as well as doing some inventive recycling. Sampling in this book is, wherever possible, a mix of recycled materials with additional bought-in items.

Recycle, unravel yarns, deconstruct weaves, and unpick braids, ribbons and edgings from worn clothing and household furnishings. Wash and over-dye uninspiring yarns and fabrics, and use some of the techniques outlined on the following pages to transform these materials into something that looks sophisticated and aesthetically desirable. The trick is to go beyond a standard recycled look. For inspiration, see the samples shown on pages 34 and 40, which were knotted in handmade cordage made from reclaimed scarves on a domestic sewing machine.

Dyeing fibres

When working from first principles, some basic knowledge of fibre properties, and the various classes of dyestuffs suitable for small-scale dyeing, are prerequisites for success. A brief overview of fibre properties followed by notes on colour mixing follows. For further information, many specialist books are available on dyeing (see Further Reading, page 124).

Textile fibres

Working with textiles demands a working knowledge of fibres from a scientific as well as an art-and-design perspective, in addition to an environmental awareness, as noted opposite.

To push the boundaries of what is possible in textile art, a combination of hands-on experimentation and creativity needs to be matched by an understanding of the physical properties of the materials being used.

This applies whether the work is made from traditional fibres or the new generation of micro-fibres such as Lutradur, Evalon and Tyvek, which possess unique and exciting characteristics for the contemporary textile artist.

Wool and silk yarns used for the knitting tubes and ties were dyed with acid dyestuffs to match the existing colour of the unspun wool tops.

These twined samples were constructed using paper tape and electrical cable. The materials were overdyed with disperse dyes to transform the off-the-shelf cable colours.

Dyeing yarns and fibres

Dyeing is both an art and a science. Traditional textile dyes would have been derived from natural sources until the late 19th century, when the first synthetic dyestuff was discovered. Today there are a number of different types of dye available to the small-scale maker for dyeing protein and cellulose fibres, as well as the more popular manmade or synthetic fibres.

Note: health and safety issues

Although no chemical should be regarded as entirely hazard-free, fabric dyes for craft purposes, and associated chemicals, present a relatively low risk. *Note that this is so long as they are handled with proper precautions, and that the manufacturer's guidelines on health and safety are adhered to.* For more advice on health and safety issues, see page 126.

Identification and classification of fibres

Natural fibres include animal, vegetable and mineral-based substances, while manmade or synthetic fibres can either be regenerated cellulose (vegetable fibre) or entirely synthetic.

Animal fibres, which are protein based, include wool and silk, and also hair fibres such as alpaca, llama, camel, goat, rabbit and dog hair. Vegetable fibres include cotton, bamboo, linen, jute, nettle, hemp and ramie.

It should be noted that there is no single class of dyestuff that will colour all fibres. If successful colouration is to take place, both the fibre and the correct dyestuff must be identified and matched for compatibility.

Dyeing techniques and dye recipes

There are many excellent books on dyeing techniques available, offering in-depth advice on any number of specialized dyeing techniques, most of which are beyond the remit of this book. Please refer to Further Reading (page 124) for suggested titles.

The dyes used for the projects in this book are available from Kemtex Educational Supplies Ltd (see Suppliers, page 124), as is a really useful set of information sheets with easy-to-understand dye recipes. These are available for the four main classes of dyestuff used in this book and include reactive dyes for the cold-water dyeing of cellulose fibres including cotton, linen and viscose rayon.

Dyes that require a hot-water dye-bath include acid dyes for protein fibres such as wool and silk, direct dyes for cotton, linen and viscose rayon, and disperse dyes for polyester and other synthetic fibres. The latter includes dyeing the plastic sleeve covering the electrical wire used in the samples shown opposite and below.

This sample is made from paper rush and electrical cable overdyed with dispersed dyes.

Disperse dyes can also be used to colour synthetics, including Lutradur, using the transfer printing process.

Dyeing undyed cordage

One method used throughout this book involves the dyeing of various combinations of yarns and fibres together in the same dye-bath.

Yarns and fibres can be pre-dyed prior to making cordage, or coloured once the cordage has been constructed. Using the latter method, many different effects can be achieved, depending upon the combination of fibres, dyestuffs and chosen dyeing method.

For example, choose to work with different textures and weights of undyed yarn, selecting either protein or cellulose-based fibres, so that they can be coloured using the same class of dyestuff. Create subtle, close hues by utilizing the natural variations in shades in the undyed colours. These different, yet related, fibres will generally dye to different depths and shades of colour, as shown in the sample below.

Ragged Sea Anemones. These coiled forms were constructed in viscose, cotton and linen fibres. The fibres were dyed in a cold-water dye bath using fibre-reactive dyes.

Practical colour mixing

Traditionally, colour mixing with paint was taught using a palette of three colour (pigment) primaries: red, yellow and blue. These three colours usually need additional pigment colours to mix a full spectrum of clear, bright shades.

However, mixing colours from a balanced set of six colours (two yellows, two blues and two reds) should give a full spectrum of hues from clear, bright colours through to neutral, dull or muted shades. Pale shades can be achieved by adding white or watering the paint down. Dark colours are mixed by blending complementary colours.

You need a yellow biased towards green (lemon yellow) and a second yellow biased towards orange (cadmium yellow). One blue should be biased towards purple (ultramarine) and the other towards green (cerulean blue). To complete the set of six colours, a red with an orange bias (cadmium red) and a red that is purple biased (magenta) are required.

Practise using the six-colour mixing system with a set of acrylic paints. The same system can be applied to inks, dyes and watercolours to achieve the colour you want. Colours and descriptive names vary between different manufacturers. Experiment with different sets of colours until you find a set you are happy with.

A selection of hand-dyed balls of 100 per cent wool fibre yarn, dyed with acid dyestuffs in a hot water dye bath. With practice you can achieve the full spectrum of colours using mixing techniques.

To create clear, bright secondary colours (asterisked in the list below), green is made from lemon yellow and cerulean blue; orange is mixed from cadmium red and cadmium yellow; purple is mixed from crimson and ultramarine. Refer to a colour circle if necessary. Excellent colour wheels are available from The Colour Wheel Company (see Suppliers, page 124).

To create dulled-down, neutralized secondary colours, mix any of the other permutations listed below. These colours are neutralized because of the presence of all three primary colours in the mixture, whereas the clear, bright secondary colours contain only two of the primary colours. All three primaries mixed together will (in theory) result in a neutral grey.

Greens
Lemon yellow plus cerulean blue *
Cadmium yellow plus cerulean blue
Lemon yellow plus ultramarine blue
Cadmium yellow plus ultramarine blue

Oranges
Cadmium yellow plus cadmium red *
Lemon yellow plus cadmium red
Lemon yellow plus crimson
Cadmium yellow plus crimson

Purples
Crimson plus ultramarine blue *
Cadmium red plus ultramarine blue
Cadmium red plus cerulean blue
Crimson plus cerulean blue

Some simple colour mixing exercises
- To change the hue, mix one colour with another. For example, start with red and add yellow in nine steps, observing the changes in hue at each stage.

- Mix greys from complementary colours: for example, start with red and gradually add small amounts of its complementary colour (green). The middle colour of this scale should be neutral grey/black.

- To make a colour lighter (tint) or darker (shade), mix white or black with full-strength colour.

- To neutralize a colour, add grey (white plus black, or a mixture of two complementary colours).

Dyeing colours using the bias system

Look for sets of dyes that will give a similar coverage of mixed colours to the paints noted opposite. If in doubt, carry out sample dyeing, and compare the brilliance of the secondary colours against the colour wheel. Remember that various companies might label similar colours with different descriptive names and vice versa – one company's ultramarine may look quite different from another's. Some dyes are labelled with codes that indicate the red or blue content, for example, or their fastness to light or washing.

From the Kemtex range of dyes, and for each of the four main classes of dyestuff, some useful dye colours are suggested below:

Cold-water reactive dyes: Kemtex Reactive Turquoise, Blue, Cerise Red, Scarlet Red, Golden Yellow and Lemon Yellow.
Acid dyes: Kemtex Acid Turquoise, Blue, Magenta, Red, Yellow and Lemon.
Disperse dyes: Kemtex Dysperse Turquoise Blue, Bright Blue, Mid Red, Scarlet Red, Golden Yellow and Mid Yellow.
Direct dyes: Kemtex Dyrect Bright Turquoise, Royal Blue, Pink Red, Scarlet Red, Buttercup Yellow and Lemon Yellow.

A page from the author's colour notebook showing how to mix tints, tones and shades without using black. These sketches, using acrylic paint, were inspired by swirling mud pools.

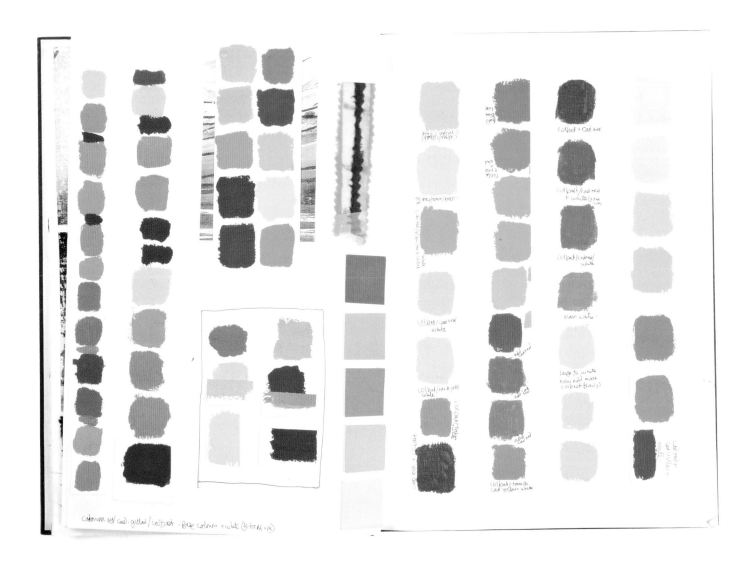

Creating a colour story or colour palette

Pages from the author's sketchbook. Acrylic paints demonstrate colour mixing from scratch using the colour bias system (see page 27).

Inspiration for colour is all around you. The trick is how to use this to your advantage as an artist. On the one hand, it is about intelligent looking and seeing to visualize how colour can inform your own artwork.

Be prepared to analyse colour combinations that appeal to your senses; for example, the relationship between one colour and another. This relationship could, for instance, be where they sit on the colour wheel, the proportion of one colour against another or the various juxtapositions of one colour next to another colour. One colour can look very different depending upon its neighbouring colour. Other factors can involve level of contrast, type of harmony and whether the colour is opaque or transparent.

Pages from the author's sketchbook showing primary research (photographs, fabrics and rubbings based on old, worn gravestones) collected as an inspirational resource for colour and texture.

An old silk scarf in soft cobalt blues, muted yellow-oranges, pale ochre, and parchment torn into strips for lengths of machine-stitched cordage could be the start of a collection of artworks using some, or all, of these colours. Over-dye orange with blue and a series of muted blue-greys, and orange-greys will be the result, depending upon the proportions and strengths of the dye colours.

Over dye the soft, cobalt blue with full-strength Ultramarine, for example, to change the intensity and hue of blue shades, or overdye yellow-orange with red-orange to change orange hues so that they become more red and less yellow. Blue and orange at full strength are complementary colours, contrasting and yet balancing each other: a colour story that suggests Australian landscapes of deep blue skies and orange soil.

Tied up in knots

Historically, knots have been used for many different purposes: to tie items together, to hold something in place, for recording and sending messages and as talismans to ward off ill fortune. Special knots are associated with particular trades and professions, for example surgeons' knots and those used in fishing and sailing.

Decorative knots

Knots are used decoratively in textile production worldwide, for example to make lace, netting and knotted edgings and fringes. All these techniques can be exploited to create exciting textile art in relief and three dimensions.

Knotting constructed with half hitches and double half hitches, along with overhand knots, form the basis for many of the simply constructed, yet effective knotted structures shown throughout this chapter.

Examples include knotting in multiples, knots worked vertically, horizontally or at an angle, knotting as a stand-alone technique, or in conjunction with coiling and other off-loom textile techniques (other examples of these techniques can also be found in the samples on pages 114 and 122, for example).

Initial experiments in this chapter cover basic knot-making techniques, to create experimental chains of knots and lengths of handmade cordage, moving on to more complex forms constructed in three dimensions around a former.

Knotting in the round. This sample features horizontal double half-hitch knots in 100 per cent linen and gimp (viscose yarn whipped around a cotton core). The knots are knotted over cotton warp yarn. The materials were piece dyed in direct dyes. This sample shows short- and full-round knotting.

Chain of knots

Making a series of half-hitch knots over the thumb or a finger can quickly and easily produce evenly spaced chains of knots along a smooth piece of string. Make sure that the knots are not too tight to take off the thumb. Gently remove the loops one by one from the thumb into a bundle, at the same time inserting the working end of the cord back up through the loops, and back out through the first loop, followed by the chain of knots. It is important to keep the loops open and to take them off the thumb in the correct sequence.

The same effect can be achieved by making a thumb cast-on over a knitting needle, or a length of dowelling, and then taking the knots off with a bodkin, which is pushed back through the knots towards the starting point.

Tie a series of overhand knots into the knotted cordage for additional textural interest, and as a way of introducing larger-scale knots into a piece of work.

Diagram 1: Lark's head (reversed double half-hitch) knot.

Half hitches and double half hitches

These simple knots involve two basic elements, one active the other passive. The core, or knot-bearing cord, is the passive element, while the active element is the flexible knot-tying cord.

A third element is the header cord, which is generally seen as a temporary holding cord, used to set out the threads before starting to knot, and then removed when the work is complete. It can also be used as an integral part of the design.

The half hitch

Refer to diagram 1 and attach a doubled-over length of cord onto a wooden rod with a lark's head knot (sometimes referred to as a reversed double half hitch). These two ends of cord are used to make the half-hitch knot as described below.

Diagram 2: Single half hitch.

Tied from left to right, the half-hitch knot is worked with these two ends of cordage (or multiples of two), where one end (A) is passive and the other (B) is active, as shown in diagrams 2 and 3. The passive cord (A) on the right is the knot-bearing cord, while the active cord (B) on the left forms the knot.

Hold cord A taut, then knot cord B around cord A by bringing B to the front of A, and up and under it. Pull the free end of the working cord tight. Continue in this manner to make a simple chain of knots. To tie from right to left, the passive cord (B) on the left is the knot-bearing cord, while the active cord (A) on the right forms the knot.

Diagram 3: Double half hitch.

Detail of a three-headed knot form (see page 122). The anchor cord used is medium-weight gimp. The knotting cords are light-weight gimp and rayon seam-binding ribbon. The materials have been piece dyed with Kemtex direct dyes.

The top two samples are chains of half-hitch knots worked alternately from the left and the right.

The two bottom samples conceal passive cores of thick sisal string, knotted over with heavyweight gimp and handmade cordage.

The top two samples shown below were made from two cords with contrasting texture. Cord A, used double, was made from reclaimed scarf fabric. This was over-stitched on a sewing machine with a fine, 0.1mm silver-coloured craft wire in the bobbin for a firm, yet flexible handle. Cord B consists of two ends of hand-dyed seam-binding tape (viscose rayon). Direct dyes were used in a hot dye-bath to achieve a good depth of colour. In these examples cords A and B take it in turns to be the active and passive elements.

Note the twist that occurs in this type of chain when the half hitch is knotted from either the left or the right throughout. A non-twisted chain will result if left and right knots are alternated. When the half hitch is worked twice, it is referred to as the double half hitch, or a clove hitch.

Working with multiple cords

Once you've mastered the basic knots you can take things further by incorporating more cords. Using multiple cords for the core (see diagram 1, right), will increase the thickness of the finished cordage and gives you the opportunity to create different effects by working on the core cords individually (see diagram 2).

You can also increase the number of active cords, as in the bottom two samples shown opposite. To make these cords you will need a minimum of two active cords for knotting (A and B), each made up of single or multiple ends. The samples shown were worked over passive cores of thick sisal string; alternatives could be washing line or sash cord. The core fibre is almost completely covered.

In these examples, two cords with contrasting texture were chosen for the active element. Cord A (doubled) is made from reclaimed scarf fabric overstitched with craft wire. Cord B is two ends of hand-dyed heavyweight Picasso Gimp, which has a beautiful sheen. Direct dyes were used in a hot dye-bath to achieve a good depth of colour.

Make the cord in half-hitch knots, selecting one cord at a time and knotting it over the core for as many knots as required. The active cord B (that is not being used to make knots) is allowed to float alongside the knots made by cord A, or concealed with the core fibre.

When one colour is about to run out, lay it parallel to the core fibre, attach the new length of cord with a lark's head (reversed double half hitch) knot around the core, and continue knotting, hiding the ends of the old cord with the half-hitch knots.

A practical tip for working with gimps: this yarn has a tendency to unravel. Wrap masking tape around the cut end, or use Fray Check or similar.

Experiments in half-hitch knotting techniques

Experiment with clustering cords together in different permutations. For example, if you start with six working cords, they can be knotted in groups of three, or subdivided into groups of two (see page 39).

More, or fewer, cords can be used as the passive core. For example, working with six cords, make a four-cord core with two cords carried together as the knotting cord, or vice versa.

Practise splitting the bundles of cords to create different thicknesses along the length of the chain, adding and subtracting cords as you go, and swapping cords between active and passive mode. An easy way to add a new length of cord is to attach a doubled-over cord with a lark's head (reverse double half-hitch) knot over the existing knotting cord at suitable intervals.

See the techniques that follow for some ideas for making a series of experimental knotted cordage.

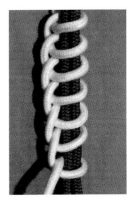

Diagram 1: Half hitch knotted from the left over a double-ended core.

Diagram 2: Half hitches knotted in series, first on one of the core cords and then on the other.

Multi-ended core

Knotted in undyed yarns, the sample shown in the background below is constructed from eight separate ends, comprising four ends of optic white, viscose chainette (cord A) and four ends of banana fibre (cord B). Suitable for dyeing with cold-water reactive dyes or hot-water direct dyes, this sample was dyed, on completion, with the latter.

All eight cords will double up as the active and passive elements as the work progresses; sometimes hidden from view when they form the core, at other times as visible elements of the design.

Work through all eight ends one after the other, as described on page 35. Repeat the process, adding new ends of yarn where required. A further option is to subdivide the eight ends into two or more parts, treating each of these subdivisions as a separate element, knotting over first one group and then the second group, until such times as they are reunited into one main cord.

This type of multiple-ended set-up allows for many more variations in thickness, splitting off and rejoining of sections. Note also that in this example, tightly tied, closely packed knots lose their definition when worked in the chainette yarn, in the same way as the rough edges of banana fibre blur the knots.

Multi-ended cores. The sample shown in the background contains eight ends doubled up as active and passive elements. The sample in the foreground contains various subdivisions of active and passive elements.

Further experiments might include adding and subtracting ends of yarn, or gradually making the cordage thinner or thicker as the work progresses. The sample shown in the foreground (left) was knotted in a wool/silk mix with viscose chainette and covered elastic, and dyed as for the previous sample. If the cordage were to be used in circular coiling, then starting thin would be advantageous for the commencement of the coiling process (see chapter 5).

The sample shown above illustrates a variety of cordage, constructed with multiple ends of paper yarns, and over-dyed with re-active dye in cold water.

Chains of knots constructed from hand-dyed paper yarns, with bamboo-cane beads.

Knotting in three dimensions

Rigid structures knotted vertically, horizontally or diagonally in double half hitches are the basis for the three-dimensional forms shown on the following pages. You can work with soft, textile-related materials that can be varnished or treated to make them hard, or use more rigid materials, such as wire and basket makers' cane.

You will need to work over a former or mould, which can be temporary or a permanent feature of the piece. An ideal temporary form for small-diameter cylindrical shapes is foam plastic water-pipe insulation, which is soft enough to pin into, yet firm and lightweight enough to make a hand-held mould. With care, the mould can be reused several times. To cut the insulation material to the right length, use a small hand-held saw, observing suitable safety procedures.

Other useful temporary forms are cardboard tubes and cones, or tall bubble-wrapped jars, for example.

Horizontal, double and half-hitch knots

Knotting in the round over a cardboard cone former.

Try a small sample based on the following instructions. Use a short length of tubular water-pipe insulation or a cardboard tube as the temporary mould.

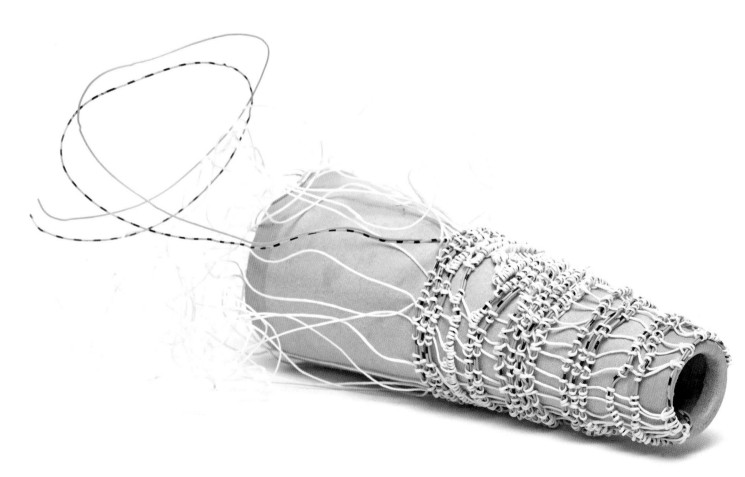

These diagrams show a series of double half-hitch knots worked in two dimensions for clarity, but the instructions explain how to work over your tube former. When working in two dimensions the anchor cord is pinned horizontally to a soft board so that it sits across the top of the vertical knotting cords.

Working in three dimensions

1. Cut ten or more lengths of strong thread (linen for example) each approximately 100cm (40in) long. Double these over at the halfway points, and mount onto a separate header cord with a lark's head (reverse double half hitch) knot. Space the cords close together for a solid design, or more widely spaced for openwork structures (see diagram 1).

2. Transfer the header cord with working cords attached, so that it encircles the top of the tube. Knot the header cord into a circle and pin in place, using a glass-headed pin. There is now a circle of 20 or more working cords, each 50cm (20in) long, hanging from the top of the tube.

3. Working from the top downwards, start the knotting process by selecting any one of the cords, and lay it at right angles over the remaining cords around the tube. This cord is now the anchor cord for the first round of knotting.

4. Select the next adjacent working cord and use this to tie a double half-hitch knot around the anchor cord (see diagrams 2 and 3). Continue to tie each working cord around the anchor cord until you reach the end of the round (see diagram 4). You can work a clockwise, or anticlockwise, pathway.

5. The second cord from the start now becomes the anchor cord for the next round. Continue to work round and round in this manner, tying in new cords as and when you need them. (On a two-dimensional form work even-numbered rows in the opposite direction as shown in diagram 5).

You can create different patterns and be creative with the knots by changing direction to create short rows (see diagrams 6, 7 and 8).

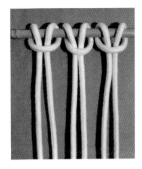

Diagram 1: Double the threads over at the halfway point with a lark's head (reversed double half-hitch) knot.

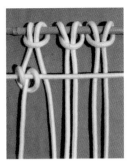

Diagram 2: Double half-hitch knots are worked in turn from left to right over the anchor cord.

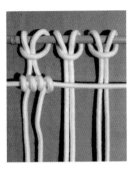

Diagram 3: The double half hitches can be knotted tightly.

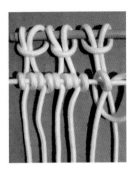

Diagram 4: Completing the first row of double half-hitch knots.

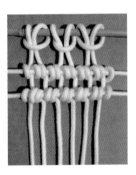

Diagram 5: Work a second row of knots from right to left.

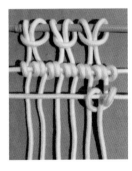

Diagram 6: Short row knotting right to left.

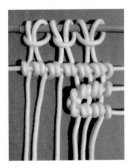

Diagram 7: Short row knotting left to right.

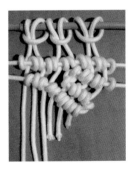

Diagram 8: Short-row knotting section completed.

An alternative working method is to use the same length of cord as the anchor cord throughout. In this example, you move from one set of working cords to the next, knotting a horizontal half-hitch over the passive anchor cord as you go, in the same way as described on page 39.

This is a good technique for introducing wire or thin cable without the need to knot it, and this can be both the header cord and the continuous length of cordage to knot over. Make sure that this is long enough to wind around the mould as many times as is needed, particularly if you are working with wire or cable. Cable is difficult to join.

The samples shown below illustrate a series of experimental forms constructed over a former and knotted in machine-stitched cordage, some of which was over-stitched with craft wire in the bobbin.

Experimental forms knotted in the round, manipulated into shape after being removed from the temporary cardboard former. The sample on the left was stitched into a closed shape, while the sample on the right was scrunched into shape.

Knotting around a cone shape

For a densely packed knotted surface, add new knotting cords as the cone shape gets wider towards the base. For a more open, linear form, keep the same number of knotting cords as were attached at the start. As the shape gets wider, there will be more space between the ties binding the piece together.

Keep turning the work around as you knot one cord after the other, knotting in a clockwise or anticlockwise direction. Interesting patterns can be worked, where partial rounds are knotted first in one direction and then the other (the sample shown on page 31, for example, was worked in this manner). The sections that stand out from the main shape were knotted back and forth, in a series of short rows.

The sample shown below shows a small, functional pouch knotted over a cardboard cone in horizontal half hitches, in dyed paper yarn over a wire core. Close one end of the tubular form by stitching across the base. The knotted cords with decorative buttons were added on completion.

Knotted pouch in wire and dyed paper string.

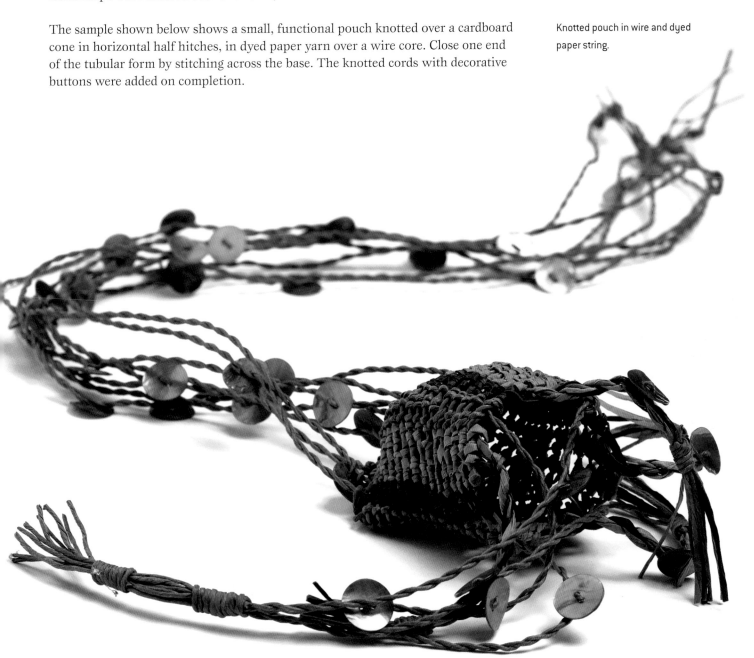

Vertical, double half-hitch knots

To make a two-dimensional sample in vertical, double half hitches, you will need to attach a series of cords to the header cord, as described on page 39. In addition to anchor cords hanging down vertically from the header cord (the passive element in this technique), you will need a long working cord to make a vertical double-hitch knot, one knot above the other, around each consecutive anchor cord, as shown right in diagrams 1–4.

To make a three-dimensional sample, try working with a widely spaced set-up for the vertical anchor cords (mediumweight gimp, Texere Yarns) attached to water-pipe insulation of 4.5cm (1in) diameter, with pins to keep the cords in position. To work in three dimensions, simply work around and around the former.

Use ten cords, each doubled over to make 20 ends in total. The holding cords can be knotted over in pairs, separated into single units for a couple of rounds and then brought back together in pairs. Add extra holding cords in the gaps to make a more densely packed structure.

Use vertical hitching for forms that are constructed partly from wire. The passive anchor cord is better suited to wire than active knotting cord because it is difficult to control the shape of a wire knot.

Incorporating objects

Choosing to incorporate an object permanently into a piece of work needs careful consideration, so that the knot patterns and the fibres reflect, or enhance, qualities of the chosen object in a visually sympathetic manner. When knotting over an irregular shape, such as a shell, you will need to add or subtract the number of anchor cords to suit the form in question.

The sample on page 88, for example, shows knotted hemp and nettle fibre, worked over a piece of driftwood. Here the idea was to construct a subtle intervention over a piece of natural form, which from a distance tantalizes the viewer into thinking that the intervention was an integral part of the found object.

Further developments might involve subverting the regularity of the knotting pattern by leaving more or less space between each round of knotting, or turning the work around and knotting back in the opposite direction at selected points in the design, adding or subtracting cords as you work. Vary the number of knots made over any given cord.

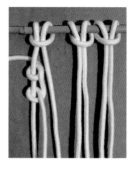

Diagram 1: A vertical double half-hitch knot.

Diagram 2: Vertical double half hitches are knotted around each consecutive anchor cord.

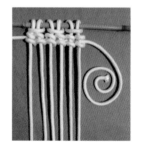

Diagram 3: A completed row of vertical half hitches.

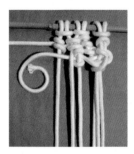

Diagram 4: The second row is worked from right to left. When working in three dimensions, keep working round and round the former in the same direction.

Combining techniques

Horizontal and vertical knots

This project shows a combination of vertical and horizontal half-hitch knots, worked over water-pipe insulation material, where blocks and stripes of colour have been achieved by exchanging active knotting cords and passive holding cords, so that they are alternately hidden or revealed, depending upon their roles. Additional cords have been added where necessary, for example to make a solid stripe of bright pink or deep blue in vertical half-hitch knots for one full round.

Contrasts in texture occur where machine-stitched cordage is placed next to one end of organza ribbon, the latter knotting up much more tightly than the cordage. The difference in the knot sizes also means that some knots stand proud of the surface. A further contrast appears between the rows of horizontally and vertically tied half-hitch knots and, of course, the contrast in colour, notably the relatively small proportion of pink in relation to the blues and greens.

Knotted pouch in horizontal and vertical half-hitch knots.

Coiled and knotted tall form

This piece is knotted over a cardboard cone, using a combination of thick and thin yarns, with contrasting smooth and rough textures in matt and sheen finishes in undyed yarns. The active cords comprise ten ends of Texere, Picasso Gimp, alternating with ten ends of rayon seam-binding tape: the anchor cord is heavy ecru Picasso Gimp viscose with a cotton core.

The tall, cylindrical form that is shown here was made in full rounds of overhand knotting and double half-hitch knots. These are combined with knotting patterns that fall short of full rounds; in some instances knotting back over part of the pathway of the preceding round, and interrupting the regularity of the surface pattern by adding, or subtracting, the number of knots made at any given point.

Knobbly overhand knots contrast with the smoother vertical columns of multiple half-hitch knot patterns. As the work progressed, so the form was unpinned and moved higher up the cardboard cone. Use glass-headed notice-board pins to secure the work to the cardboard at intervals, particularly at the points where the form is turned to work back in the opposite direction.

Knotted in three dimensions, this tall form combines full and partial rounds of knotting. Tails of seam-binding ribbon were added on completion of the knotting. This piece was dyed with Kemtex direct dyes.

Three-headed form

Three-dimensional knotting techniques were combined with a base constructed using a radial coiling technique (see chapter 5) to make a seemingly complex structure, a detail of which is shown below. It was, however, built from individual units where each unit is similar, but not identical. This repetition of related shapes helps to unify the design visually. See the finished piece on page 122.

To make a similar form, first knot three or more free-standing cylinders in open and closed knotting patterns around the wide end of a cardboard cone shape.

Remove the knotting from the cardboard form, leaving the tails from the knotting cords in place. Commence working rounds of radial coiling as explained in chapter 5, using the tails from the three-dimensional knotting as the knotting cords. The anchor cord continues as before, but is manipulated to make a flat surface, following the contours of the base of the cylinder.

Use the remaining lengths of knotting cords to join individual cylinders one to another, knotting up through the open spaces of one cylinder with a cord from another. Add more cords where necessary, or eliminate redundant cords at a suitable point in the work.

The anchor cord is Texere Picasso Gimp, a viscose yarn with a cotton core in optic white. The knotting cords are a combination of Texere Picasso Gimp in fine ecru, and winter white Hug Snug viscose seam-binding tape from Lawrence Schiff Silk Mills (see Suppliers, page 124) and piece-dyed with direct dye.

To construct a larger piece, repeat the three-piece module several times over. Join these larger units together, in the manner described above. Consider changing the scale and the materials used in some of these units to add visual contrast: an important element in all design work.

Detail of three-headed knotted form. The anchor cord is of mediumweight light gimp, while the knotting cords are a lightweight gimp and rayon seam binding.

All wrapped up

Wrapping and binding fibres or strips of textiles around themselves can be a simple yet effective technique to give rigidity and strength to otherwise fragile or flexible fibres. It is an equally effective way of holding bundles of fibres together, and can be used as a method of protection from external elements.

Traditional uses for wrapping

In ancient times strips of linen were used to wrap and protect Egyptian mummies. The linen was painted with a liquid resin to glue the wrapped bandages together. Linen was chosen for its strength and suppleness, and its ability to retain its shape due to its inherent inelasticity. Linen will also absorb moisture yet still feel dry.

Traditional basketry techniques utilized a core of wrapped fibres stitched into coils to make functional and ceremonial baskets, plaques, water-tight containers (treated with pitch) and even floor coverings.

Hand-dyed paper yarn, hand wrapped around a core of twisted paper string.

Using a quite different approach, ceremonial body armours from Sepik in New Guinea were constructed using similar basketry techniques in wrapped fibres, which were treated with clay. Today, boxers might wrap their hands and wrists in fabric strips to protect them from injury in boxing.

For the textile artist, wrapping and binding techniques can be used to create structural elements in fibre, making fragile materials strong or creating purely decorative effects where fibres are wrapped over an existing shape in colourful patterns and textures.

In this chapter, the main focus is on colourful wrappings suitable for small-scale jewellery projects, embellishments for home décor and for personal apparel, and covers both structural and decorative techniques.

Further examples of wrapping techniques can be found in chapter 9, where various small-scale, three-dimensional wrapped forms, inspired by patterns in the landscape, are illustrated.

Wrapping and binding techniques

Hand-wrapped cordage

The technique of hand-wrapped cordage involves winding thread at right angles around a core thread or threads. Commercially produced examples include gimp thread, made by wrapping silk or gold threads around a cotton core, and millinery wire – wire wrapped with paper, cotton or rayon threads to create a smooth outer surface.

Hand-wrapped cordage mimics the way these commercial examples are produced. Simply wind round and round the core (the passive element) with another thread (the active element), keeping the turns neatly adjacent to each other. The core fibres need to be kept under tension. See diagrams 1 and 2, shown right.

For short lengths of cordage use a wooden frame; for longer lengths the core fibres can be tied, or clamped, between two stationary points. Many of the samples in this chapter were clamped to a worktop and held under tension with the left hand while wrapping with the right hand (or vice versa).

Experiment with making short lengths of cordage, using regularly spaced bindings over a variety of cores, for example sisal string, bundles of high-twist rug yarn, washing line and thick rope or paper cord. Try making the bindings with a range of fibres, for example wool, ribbons, reclaimed fabric made into bias strips or paper string.

The sample shown opposite shows paper cord that has been wrapped with hand-dyed paper string. Spaces are left between successive bindings.

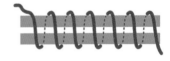

Diagram 1: Winding thread at right angles around a single core.

Diagram 2: Winding thread at right angles around a multiple core.

Figure-of-eight wrap

The samples below show linen yarn wrapped tightly over a core of thick cotton. These examples were piece-dyed with direct dyes.

To make an example similar to sample A, bind mediumweight linen yarn over four separate ends of cotton cord (Texere Yarns). Successive bindings are used to link selected areas of the cotton cord together, using a figure-of-eight wrap (see diagrams 1 and 2, right). A looped shape can be made by laying a longer section of wrapped cordage alongside a shorter section, and then binding the two together again.

Sample B shows how to develop the previous sample into a long, curvilinear three-dimensional form where successive loops are made as described above. The section of cordage that is used to make the loops will run out more quickly than the other length. Simply join in extra wrapping yarn to extend the cordage. To avoid breaks in the core fibre, do not cut it down to size until the piece has been completed.

A series of consecutive loops pointing first to the right and then the left gives a more formal interpretation of this loop-making technique. To make a similar sample, first wrap thick linen thread around a cotton core. A second line of figure-of-eight wraps is made down the centre of the piece to draw the loops up into place.

Interestingly, although the wrapped cordage is very firm, it is also quite flexible and bends into curvilinear shapes quite easily (see also samples on pages 116 and 126).

Note that linen is a relatively heavy yarn; a factor that must be accounted for if the items are to be developed into large-scale pieces.

Diagram 1: Figure-of-eight wrap showing the pathway of the wrapping yarn.

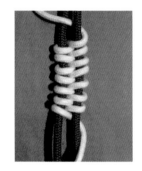

Diagram 2: Figure-of-eight wrap showing closely packed wrapping.

A

B

Sample A, shown in the background, features four separate cords, wrapped and interlinked at intervals using a figure-of-eight binding. Sample B in the foreground shows wrapped and looped bindings, where heavyweight linen yarn is wrapped over a cotton core.

Making the fragile strong

Unspun wool tops used without further processing, such as twisting, plying and spinning, are fragile and pull apart easily. By wrapping and binding them into bundles a more robust cord is made, suited to decorative applications where strength is not an issue, such as embellishments, buttons and brooches.

To make decorative cordage from unspun tops, use strong yarn such as mercerized cotton, spun silk or wool-and-silk mix as the binding element. For the examples shown below, fine mercerized crochet cotton was used. Tie a series of half-hitch knots (see page 33), one after the other from left to right over the core of unspun fibres. Leave gaps so that the colours of the core fibres show through.

To do this, attach the length of tops and yarn to a G-clamp, or mount onto a temporary header cord, a length of dowelling or similar. The bundle of tops is the passive element (cord A) and the strong thread the active element (cord B). Tie B around A, holding the latter reasonably taut, twisting the bundle of tops from time to time with one hand and knotting with the other hand. The twist will give strength to the unspun tops as it would if spinning from first principles.

As the bundle of tops runs out, allow it to taper off. Overlap a new tapered bundle of fibres parallel to the first, and continue knotting over it. Use this method of working to introduce new colours, or for adding and subtracting fibres to the core to vary the thickness. You can also introduce different types of fibre.

A simple method of adding in new binder thread, if it is double stranded or more, is to attach the new length of yarn using a lark's head (reversed double half hitch) knot (see page 33), just as you would mount the active cord over the header cord in knotting projects. Disguise the old ends in the core fibres as you knot.

Commercially dyed wool tops bound with fine mercerised cotton (left) and wool and silk fibres (right), plied with fine metal thread.

Consider varying the spacing of the knots and working with more than one end of knotting yarn. The knotting yarn can be knotted over the core in any number of different permutations. For example, work the knots alternately from left to right in the first colour, and right to left in the second colour. You could add lengths of fine, glittery fibres to the core for contrast, or wrap the fibre bundle in wire.

Two-dimensional surfaces

This technique combines wrapping and knots. A continuous length of wrapped cordage is knotted together row after row, with chains of knots tied at right angles to the cordage. The instructions given below are for a rectangular two-dimensional surface, which is further developed into three-dimensional coiled forms in chapter 5 (see diagrams, page 70).

To create a similar piece, make a long length of wrapped unspun tops as described on page 49. The length can be added to as the work progresses.

The next step involves knotting the wrapped tops into a single surface. To do this, cut an even number of lengths of knotting cord in a suitable fibre or alternative linear material. For this example a fine, enamelled copper craft wire was used.

1. Work on a flat surface. Find the middle of each of the knotting cords, double them over and knot them over the wrapped cordage with a lark's head (reversed double half-hitch) knot (see page 33), working from left to right and starting from the short end. Space the knotting cords evenly along the cordage, noting that the length of the start is determined by the measurement of one side of the rectangle.

Detail showing thick and thin bindings with various spacings, wrapped over commercially dyed wool tops.

Knotted and wrapped surface. In this example the knotting material is 0.2mm enamelled craft wire.

2. Bend the long end of the wrapped cordage back on itself, so that it faces in the opposite direction, parallel to the first row. In the next step the knotting cords are used to join this second row of wrapped cordage to the first row.

3. Working from right to left, select each pair of knotting cords in turn. One end goes under the fibre bundle and the other end over the top of the core. Knot these two ends together using overhand knots, so that the wrapped cordage core is firmly tied in between the knotting cords. Move on to the next pair of ends and perform the same task until the end of the row is reached.

4. Continue working in this manner, knotting each length of wrapped tops to the previous one for a regular-shaped surface. Alternatively, interrupt the regularity of the knotted rows by working short rows. Experiment with the spacing of the knotting cords, introducing or eliminating pairs of knotting cords as the work progresses.

More ideas with unspun wool tops

This series of decorative circles was constructed from off-the-shelf, dyed, unspun wool tops bound with fine mercerized cotton, craft wire and glitter thread.

To make these circles, tease out a beginning and end from a bundle of fibres to make an inconspicuous join. Wrap the fibres around a ring stick (or dowel) for a minimum of three turns, ensuring that the fibres are running parallel to each other and overlapping the tapered ends.

Commence the stitching to one side of this overlapping section, using a flat bodkin to push any stray ends of fibres to the underneath of the circle. Make the first round of stitching widely spaced, but close enough to secure the bundle of fibres. Disguise the loose end of thread in the next round or secure on the back with a small knot.

For additional colour and decoration, make more than one binding. Remove the coil from the ring stick. Add a second round (or subsequent rounds) in a contrasting colour, or different type or thickness of fibre, perhaps leaving some of the core of the second round visible. Use buttonhole stitches on the edge of a coil as a purely decorative feature.

Various size circles of wrapped wool tops. Each circle is constructed around a ring stick, stitched together one inside the other, or piled on top of each other.

Wrapping experiments

Work with handmade cordage to create decorative items, such as this prototype for a rope necklace, shown below, which is constructed from machine-stitched cordage and contrasting bindings.

Multiple bindings one on top of the other offer unlimited potential for varying the textures and colour combinations. For example you could bind over a thick cord with a thinner thread, allowing the core fibres and the original binding to show through in selected areas.

Add a further layer of cross wrappings over the original bindings to create a variety of surface patterns and textural contrasts, working with wire and glitter yarns, or smooth and textured silks, banana fibre yarn or hand-dyed hemp yarn.

Leave areas of the core fibres unwrapped, allowing them to balloon out. Visually this works particularly well where there is a strong surface contrast, for example hair fibres wrapped with spun silk. Add and subtract fibres from the core elements to make fatter or thinner wraps, while varying the fibres and textiles used for binding.

Further embellish hand-wrapped cordage by adding beads, buttons, sequins and other found objects. To incorporate feathers into the bindings, simply trim the feathery section off from the central spine of the feather, leaving a long enough length to wrap into the bindings. To do this, lay the exposed central spine of the feather parallel to the core and proceed to cover it.

Prototype for a rope necklace in machine-stitched cordage and contrasting bindings.

A practical tip: remember to secure the ends of the wrapping threads using one of the techniques outlined on page 57. If this is not possible due to the nature of the wrapping threads, as a last resort a glue gun can be used discreetly.

Making decorative beads

Small-scale experiments with wrapping can be a useful method of making decorative fabric and thread beads. These can be incorporated into many of the techniques covered in this book.

Colourful beads can be made by working over short lengths of polythene or cardboard tube. In the examples shown below, a mix of fibres, ribbons and wire is used to wrap the tubes with layered multiple bindings. Turn to page 57 to find out how to secure the ends of the bindings.

Sample beads

To make a sample bead, first cut a length of thread such that it will closely cover the plastic tube. To determine the length, make a temporary wrapping of the thread around the tube, unwind the wrapping and take a measurement. Add extra for tails (which will be hidden in the wrapping at the beginning and end of each bead).

To wrap a tube 2.5–3cm (1–1¼in) long and 0.5cm in diameter, a cut length of 60cm (24in) of thread was sufficient for the example shown below. Remember that thicker or thinner thread will be comparatively shorter or longer in length.

Decorative beads. These are made from clear polythene tubes wrapped with glitter thread and assorted yarns.

To make the first wrappings, use a hot-glue gun to stick the end of the thread to the tube a little way in from the cut end of the tube so that it will be eventually hidden beneath the bindings. Alternatively, use a length of masking tape or invisible tape. Keep flat bodkins conveniently to hand – you can use them to secure the end of thread through the bindings, as described in method 3 (opposite). Wrap the thread tightly around the tube from right to left until you reach the halfway point.

Lay the flat bodkin parallel to the tube with the eye pointing to the left. Continue to wrap around the tube and the bodkin until you reach the other end, making sure the eye of the bodkin is left unwrapped. Thread the remainder of the wrapping thread through the eye of the bodkin, and pull through the bindings.

Note that half of the bodkin should be left unwrapped so that it can be pulled through the bindings from the right-hand side. For longer tubes, introduce the bodkin at a later point or it will be impossible to pull through the bindings.

The second and subsequent layers can be secured using a length of linen thread as a temporary 'needle', as described in method 3. A closer wrapping can be made using thread rather than a needle, but that can be difficult to manipulate on the first layer over the polythene tube.

The sample below shows the bead-making technique worked on a larger scale over cardboard tubes that have been wrapped with multiple bindings as described above, and strung together using the onion-stringing technique outlined in chapter 8.

Cardboard tubes wrapped with 2- and 3-ply cordage and organza ribbon. The tubes are strung together over a thicker central cord (see stringing objects onion style on page 112).

Securing the wrapping yarn

There are several effective methods for securing the tails of the wrapping yarn, working with and without the use of a needle. Choice of working method should be determined by the strength of the wrapping yarn, the length of the wrapped section, and the types of yarns and fibres used for the core and bindings.

Method 1

Lay the tail of the wrapping yarn parallel to the core from left to right, and then start wrapping back over the core and the tail of yarn from right to left (see diagram 1). To secure the other end, make a loop with the remaining part of the tail, and lay this parallel to the core (see diagram 2). Wrap around the core and the extra tails of yarn towards the loop. Insert the wrapping yarn through the loop (see diagram 3). Pull taut so that the wrapping yarn travels down through the bindings. Cut off the tail ends.

Method 2

The second method is to use a large-eyed, flat bodkin to pull the wrapping yarn through the bindings. This method works best with short sections of wrapping and where the wrapping yarn is thin enough to go through the eye of the needle. Thread up the needle and pull the wrapping thread all the way through the complete length of the binding, tightening the coil by twisting the needle gently. Cut off the tail ends of yarn.

Method 3

Begin by laying the wrapping yarn from left to right, parallel with a length of solid core, such as washing line. Now wrap back over the core from right to left, over the yarn and the long tail end. Arrange the wrapping yarn at right angles to the core before you start binding back towards the left. Wrap tightly and evenly.

At the midway point of the bindings, lay a flat bodkin or a loop of strong yarn over the remainder of the core yarn. The loop or eye of the needle should point to the left, with the two loose ends of the loop of fibre pointing towards the right, overlapping the area you have just wrapped. Continue binding the core and the loop/needle as one. When the wrapping is completed, use the loop from the auxiliary yarn to pull the tail end of the wrapping yarn through the bindings to secure it. Insert the tail end of the wrapping yarn through the loop, while keeping your finger on the binding to stop it coming undone. Pull both ends of the auxiliary yarn to the right to draw the wrapping yarn under the binding from left to right. Cut off the loose tail ends.

Method 4

The final method, based on Peruvian wrapping techniques, uses a U-shaped loop made in the actual wrapping yarn to draw the end through the binding. Use a strong yarn to wrap with, or it will break when you pull the end through. Lay the wrapping yarn parallel to the core in a U-shape (see diagram 4). Hold the core thread in the left hand, and start wrapping with the right hand over the core and towards the U (see diagram 5). Once you have completed wrapping, insert the end of yarn you have been wrapping with through the U-shaped loop and hold it tight. Pull the end of yarn protruding from the right-hand end of the wrapped section so that the left end of the wrapping yarn is drawn up through the wrapped section to secure it tightly. You will feel the end travelling up through the wrapping if you have done this manoeuvre correctly.

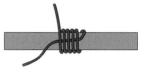

Diagram 1: Wrapping back over the core and the tail of yarn from right to left.

Diagram 2: Making a loop with the remaining part of the tail.

Diagram 3: Loop waiting for wrapping yarn to be inserted.

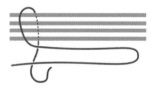

Diagram 4: Lay the wrapping yarn parallel to the core in a U shape.

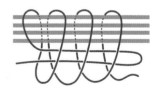

Diagram 5: Peruvian wrapping method.

Taking it forward

Wrapping is an essential part of the coiling process and one that is described in more detail in chapter 5 and explored further in chapter 9.

The samples shown here illustrate decorative wrapping techniques while at the same time demonstrate how stitching techniques can be used to join one section of a coil to the next. The techniques are suitable for small-scale embellishments and personal adornment.

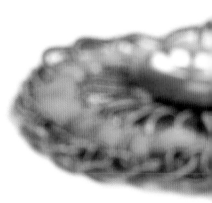

Going around in circles

Generally associated with traditional basket making, coiling techniques involve winding a continuous foundation core into a spiral or some other shape, where each new round is bound to the previous one by thinner, more flexible fibres.

Crossovers and blurred distinctions

The foundation core is the passive element, analogous to the role of warp threads in weaving; the active element is the process of binding, wrapping, stitching and knotting one section of the coil to the next.

There are many crossovers and blurred distinctions between coiling and the wrapping techniques described in chapter 4. Similarly, radial coiling combines coiling with knotting as described in chapter 3. As with all of the techniques covered in this book, boundaries between one technique and another are not intended to be rigid, but are simply given as a way of organizing the contents logically, and so that the reader can make crossovers between one technique and another as the need arises.

Picking up from where chapter 4 left off, this chapter describes how decorated cordage is sampled using an overlay technique. Further experiments with wrapped circles are developed into linear, openwork forms. Techniques for making curvilinear three-dimensional forms are explored, developing coiling and wrapping techniques worked over a core of fibres, linked by various stitching techniques.

Applicable to all of the techniques is a review of suitable material for the core, and the active stitching and binding element. This chapter starts with selecting the right materials.

Choosing suitable materials

Core fibres

In traditional coiled basketry, materials such as willow rods, grasses and pine needles that were local to the region of production were used for the core. These lengths of fibrous matter were continually added to the core as the work progressed.

In the hands of the contemporary textile artist, the core materials can be chosen from a wide range of natural or synthetic fibres, provided that these are reasonably firm and flexible enough to bend and curve into shape.

The type of stitches chosen to bind the core together into a coil, and the density of stitching, determines whether the core is partially exposed, or completely concealed by the binding material.

If the core is to be totally hidden from view, then choose a single length of rope (washing line or sash cord for example) in one long continuous piece, or bundle together several ends of tightly twisted carpet wool. You can use up scrap yarn because colour is not going to be a consideration.

Experiment freely with unspun wool, silk or cotton tops, wire tubes, stuffed fabric tubes, handmade cordage, transparent plastic casing filled with fibres, fabrics and meshes rolled into tubes, plastic tubing or bundles of wrapped fabric strips if the core is to be visible.

Stitching and binding fibres

Strong, flexible thread that will go through the eye of a needle or bodkin is needed for binding and stitching the coils of fibres to each other. For example, waxed linen thread, mercerized cotton, silk, paper yarn, fine strands of leather, gimp, seam binding tape and thin ribbon can all be utilized.

Radial coiling technique. In these samples, commercially knitted wire tubes are filled with coloured wool tops and ruched cordage and then knotted together with leather suede, and hand-dyed gimp.

Strong mercerized cotton, or perhaps waxed linen thread, is a particularly suitable fibre for sewing coils together for sculptural pieces. Strong and pliable, it has a good breaking strength so that the stitches can be drawn up tightly, helping even the most asymmetrical pieces keep their structural integrity (see the sample on page 116, for example). Linen thread can be waxed by running it over a candle, making it easier to stitch with, and less likely to shred and fray.

The downside of linen is that it is a relatively heavy fibre when compared to, for example, loosely spun wool, and could impact on how the end product might be used, especially if it is a large-scale piece with all component parts of linen.

To coil in a spiral, use a flat bodkin with a large eye to stitch with: one with an angled section at the tip makes it easier to stitch coils together. For the radial coiling technique, strong binding threads are knotted around the core fibres without the need for a bodkin.

Modular constructions

To make the long frond-like cordage shown below, first construct the necessary number of wrapped circles, leaving a good length of wrapping thread hanging if the intention is to wrap the circles onto completed cordage.

For the sample shown below, tightly packed bindings, wrapped adjacent to one another so that the core fibres were completely disguised, were made in 100 per cent silk, 100 per cent wool and a wool and silk mix piece dyed with acid dyes.

Make a separate length of wrapped cordage in the same materials. Either bind in the circles at the same time as making the cordage or attach them afterwards using the length of thread left hanging from the circles.

Various sizes of wrapped circles, bound into lengths of wool and silk cordage.

The latter method works well for pieces constructed over a three-dimensional form, as shown in the next set of samples, which were made using a cardboard cone as a temporary former.

Three modular forms, constructed from individually wrapped circles in various sizes. The forms are made with hand-dyed silk.

The next group of samples shows a series of small, composite forms constructed from individually made circles, using the couronne or ring stick as a temporary former (see page 9).

To make the modular constructions shown on this page, pin the circles in place to establish a pleasing composition, paying particular attention to the way the negative and positive spaces interrelate in the round. Observe the composition from all angles. Once happy with the outcome, stitch the form together using figure-of-eight wraps or blanket stitches.

Note that sometimes the larger-sized detached circles can have a tendency to twist and turn, usually when the bundle of core fibres is too thin in relation to the strength and weight of the stitching element. A thick core combined with a thin working thread can be used to cancel out the twist, although this in turn will depend on the relative harshness or softness of both the core and binder threads. Another option is to stabilize individual coils, using the figure-of-eight wrap to bind large coils to the next size down.

Join individually wrapped circles to make more complex structures, like this modular construction in hand-dyed wool.

Stitching over a core of fibres

As noted at the beginning of this chapter, coiling is generally associated with basket making. A continuous foundation core is wound into a spiral, or perhaps some other shape. Each new round is stitched to the previous one with a thinner, more flexible fibre using a selection of stitches outlined on the following pages.

A number of different stitches are used to join one section of the coil to the next and include, for example, various methods of wrapping one coil to the next, interlocking loop stitches, openwork stitches, split stitches and decorative stitches.

In traditional coiled basketry the sewing material is stitched around, or through, the core in different pathways and patterns; sometimes the stitching is very compact and the core hidden, and in other instances the stitching is made much further apart.

Various combinations of stitch and core materials will affect the rigidity of the structure. It is here that the textile artist might want to start exploring just what is possible using this technique, to produce a more contemporary interpretation of this ancient construction method.

Practise making these stitches in two dimensions as shown opposite and on page 66, which illustrate a few working methods from which many variations can be developed. The diagrams assume the stitches are worked back and forth in two dimensions.

Use any of the core fibres suggested on pages 60–61, or experiment with any flat profile material that will allow holes to be punched into it and that will wrap easily, such as Pelmet (Craft) Vilene, flat basketry rattan or stiffened fabric. For three-dimensional coiling, use the diagrams as a guide and simply continue to stitch round and round.

Used in conjunction with the various coiling stitches, outlined below, are the wrapping and binding of core fibres as described in chapter 4. In this context this means winding the stitching fibre from front to back (or vice versa) around the core to cover it, before making a linking stitch into the previous core.

Stitch and bind

Known as lazy stitch, this method of stitching one core to another makes for a fairly loose structure when compared with a figure-of-eight wrap, and is a simple wrap and stitch sequence (see diagram 1, left). To sample this stitch in two dimensions, first wrap a length of core material continuously from front to back (top to bottom) for the length of the first row with the weft thread.

On the next row, wind the thread around the core four times, for example, then bring it over from the back as before, but this time stitch around both cores, pulling taut and holding the thread in place before repeating the process. When working in the round, the number of windings between the lazy stitches can be increased, or extra stitches added as the diameter of the coil increases.

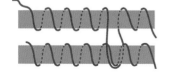

Diagram 1: Lazy stitch.

Interlocking wrapped stitches

For this technique, which can be worked over any number of different foundation cores, the stitches interlock but do not pass through the core fibres.

Take a length of thick string or rope, and wrap yarn around for 10–15cm (4–6in). Turn it back on itself so that it lies parallel to the first row. Stitch through the heads of the equivalent stitches on the first row, so as to interlock them with this new row, as shown in diagram 2, right. Try this stitch with bundles of high-twist wool for the core and a single end for stitching. Carpet yarn or similar is good for this purpose.

An alternative version assumes two elements for the core, for example two strands of thick rope. Wrap strong yarns over the latter as described above, and pull the stitches relatively tight so as to hold the two core elements together. On the next row, stitch over and under the top section of the previous row, and over and under the core. Vary the pathway of the stitching by stitching over and under the new core.

Stitches can also be looped and interlocked around a core. To do this, loop the yarn around the core as shown in diagram 3 (right) then on the next row, loop the new stitch through the bar of the loop on the preceding row and then make a loop around the new core.

Figure-of-eight stitches

The figure-of-eight stitch is a strong, joining stitch, in which the weft is wrapped around the core for several windings, as for the sample below. Here, the weft is inserted between the coils rather than spanning the two coils being joined. The weft is brought to the front from the back, then taken over, around and behind both cores, and up again then through the gap between the two cores being joined. Diagram 4 (right) shows a simplified version of the pathway this stitch takes.

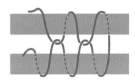

Diagram 2: Interlocked stitches.

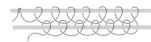

Diagram 3: Looped stitches.

Diagram 4: Figure-of-eight stitching technique.

Coiled form made from dyed paper yarn wrapped around a clear polythene tube. Wrapping, figure-of-eight stitches and knotted figure-of-eight stitches are all used to construct the sample.

Split stitches

Here, the corresponding stitches on the previous row are pierced through their centres by the needle as it makes the new stitch for the next row of coiling (see the diagram, right). If the weft is made from two ends of thread worked as one, then the needle can be pushed in between these two threads for a similar effect.

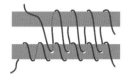

Diagram 1: Split stitches.

Openwork stitches

An openwork stitch is a development of lazy stitch or the figure-of-eight stitch, whereby a knot or a series of wraps is made around the weft in between the two cores, before recommencing the binding and stitching sequence. The more wraps or knots, the greater is the distance between one core and the next. A bead or similar object can be threaded onto the weft to achieve the same purpose.

Non-functional stitches

The samples shown below and opposite give you an idea of how you might set about embellishing the surface of your coiled forms. These include overlays and decorative stitching, incorporating add-ons such as beads and feathers or changing colours to create patterns.

Overlays

Overlaying additional materials can be used to add extra colour and texture to embellish coiled and wrapped forms; a technique sometimes referred to as 'imbrication' in traditional coiled basketry.

To make an overlay, you'll need an additional strip of material in a different texture or colour to lay alongside the core fibres and a yarn for linking these two components together. This type of decoration can be incorporated as an integral part of the making process, or added to the surface of the piece afterwards.

Both these samples are constructed from a cotton fibre core wrapped with gimp. The overlay for the sample on the left is rayon seam binding ribbon, while for the sample on the right the overlay is textured fibre seam binding tape.

The principle of making an overlay is the same for working in two or three dimensions. This first set of directions describes how to overlay a single core of fibres.

Lay the core fibres and the overlay parallel to each other, and wrap as one unit for a given length with the binding thread. Hold the overlay away from the core, continuing to bind around the core fibres only. At a suitable point, bring the overlay back into place and wrap the two elements as one again.

Further experimentation might involve making the overlay stand proud of the bindings, like a series of upstanding pleats. To do this, make the overlay material longer than the section of core fibre between each of the bindings. The bindings can be made at regular intervals or you could experiment with varying the height or distance between each pleat. When made close together and one row after another, they can resemble shingled tiles.

To incorporate this technique as an integral part of the coiling process, the additional material is laid alongside the core and caught in with the weft stitches, which link one coil to the next. To add the decoration over the top of a finished structure, various stitches can be used to apply the overlay, including split stitches (see samples on pages 14, 15 and 24, for example).

Decorative stitching

This sample is constructed from a cotton core wrapped with linen. The overlay is Tyvek fabric.

Although usually associated with embroidery, blanket stitch can be used as a decorative finish or to wrap fragile hair fibres into a robust circle, for example (see the sample on pages 52–53). The pathway the thread takes in blanket stitch is the same as the half-hitch knot worked over a cord, which is why a chain of half hitches is sometimes referred to as a buttonhole bar.

Coiling in the round

Refer to the diagrams shown right and make a practice sampler with thick carpet yarn or similar, using multiple strands for the core and a single strand for the stitching.

Tie a single length of yarn around a bundle of core fibres approximately 5cm (2in) from the end. Stagger the lengths of each of the individual pieces of core yarn so that you have a tapered end. Leave a 5cm (2in) tail of thread. Begin by wrapping this single length of thread towards the tapered end, including the tail of the stitching thread in the bindings. Wrap to within 1cm (½in) of the end (see diagram 1).

Bend the wrapped bundle of yarn back on itself to make a loop. Thread a bodkin with the stitching yarn to close and secure the newly made loop with a figure-of-eight wrap (see diagram 2). Continue to wrap over the core and the remains of the tapered end, making another figure-of-eight wrap until the latter is totally secure.

Keep bending the core round to form a coil, holding the core yarns with the left hand, and binding with a figure-of-eight stitch. Secure the working thread tightly around the core fibres with the right hand until you have two complete coils. Work anticlockwise around the coil, stitching from front to back with the core fibres pointing to the left for the right-handed worker. Reverse the instructions if left-handed.

Diagram 1: Wrapping the core fibres from left to right.

Diagram 2: Commencing the coil and securing with a sturdy figure-of-eight wrap.

The beginning of three different circular coiling projects. The sample on the left is an asymmetrical coil that combines full and partial rounds of stitching. In the centre is a standard coil of viscose ribbon and gimp, while the sample on the right is constructed from a cotton core, wrapped with linen and stitched with gimp.

From here on, attach the bound core to the preceding coil at regular intervals. Select stitches for their functional, as well as decorative, properties: the figure-of-eight wrap is a strong linking stitch; lazy stitch is not as strong, but is less time-consuming to work.

Various shapes, such as ovals, squares and asymmetrical shapes, can be developed using the directions outlined above (see the sample opposite, for example).

Moving into three dimensions

Thinking and making in three dimensions from first principles requires that you visualise the piece from all angles, either building the form from component parts, or constructing the work in the round from the very beginning of the making process.

The first method involves making a series of flat shapes that can be manipulated and linked using various methods, in much the same way that you would stitch together the component parts of a dress or skirt from flat pattern pieces.

Think of the second method in the same way as a ceramicist might make a coiled form, modelling and building the shape from clay as the work progresses.

Coiling in three dimensions

Cylindrical shapes with a circular base are an extension of the flat base shape. To work upwards into a cylindrical shape, simply lay the core fibres on top of the preceding coil rather than to one side, prior to knotting or stitching them together. This principle is applicable to all of the coiling techniques outlined above.

Asymmetrical shapes can be worked by making only a partial round or coiling, before bending the core back on itself and continuing to work back in the opposite direction. Additional segments can be designed to extend the form outwards. For example a new set of working cords can be tied into the main body of work as in the sample below and at the top of page 117.

Asymmetrical coil made with hand-dyed paper yarn (see also the finished piece on page 117).

Radial coiling

For the radial coiling technique, a number of strong binding threads are knotted around the core fibres to bind one coil to the next. Circles, ovals, spirals and asymmetrical shapes in two and three dimensions are all possible with this versatile method. The core fibres are visible in between the chains of knots, which radiate outwards like spokes in a wheel. As the coiled shapes grow larger, more binding cords are added.

A simple experiment in two dimensions with wrapped wool tops and 0.2mm enamelled copper craft wire is shown on pages 52–53.

To make circular or oval-shaped bases, follow the set-up instructions for two-dimensional sampling, noting that the length of the set-up row is dictated by the overall shape of the piece, which in this example is a long, oval shape. A circular shape would require a shorter set-up row, with only a few knotting cords by comparison.

Lay out the core fibres with the knotted-on cords so that pairs of ends point alternately to the left and right (see diagram 1). Coil the core fibres all the way around the start of the core, which contains the knotted-on cords. Select each pair of knotting cords in turn, and knot around the adjacent core (see diagram 2). The first row is quite hard to control, particularly when soft fibres are being used.

A slightly different approach can be employed for the first round. Open out all of the pairs of knotting cords pointing to the right (for example). Lay down the core all the way along this section, before tying the knots for this first half of the oval coil. Do the same for the other half of the first round of coiling. Once the start has been worked, select each pair of cords for knotting on an individual basis.

As the shape grows in size, add in more knotting cords using a lark's head (reversed double half-hitch) knot (see page 33). Pay particular attention to curves where the edges of the shape grow quickly in circumference. Additional tying cords are required here if the shape is to hold together.

Three dimensions

Move into three dimensions by laying the core on top of the previous round as opposed to adjacent to it, keeping the knot-tying cords in the correct position. Make asymmetrical and free-form shapes, coiling full and partial rounds to interrupt the regularity of the emerging shape (see samples opposite and on page 114).

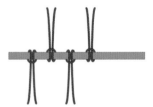

Diagram 1: Knotted on cords over core fibres.

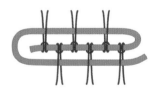

Diagram 2: Knotted on cords ready to be tied around the core fibres.

Further experimentation

Experiment with colour and pattern; make changes to core fibres and knotting cords. Combine radial coiling with detached circles, for example, or drill holes into natural forms and extend their shape with coiled sections.

Piece-dyed coiled forms or their individual components can be seen in the samples on pages 32 and 122, for example. Here, careful consideration must be given to the various combinations of fibres used in their construction and choice of dyestuff. You should always test-dye a small sample prior to making the finished piece.

Radically change the look of a piece by covering some or all of the work with plaster. Harden the fabrics with formulas such as Paverpol (see page 95), or coat with PVA or shellac varnish (French polish), taking care to follow all the health and safety guidelines associated with these different products.

Coiled textile fibres incorporating patches of metal are another option. Punch holes around the edges of metal shapes, perhaps recycled metal from drinks cans or lids that can be perforated so that threads can be attached for further experiments in radial coiling techniques.

Samples on pages 14 and 15, for example, are small rag pots constructed from a core of wrapped fabric strips with torn edges, dyed in acid dyes prior to constructing the pieces. The binding material was machine-stitched cordage made from reclaimed fabrics. Here, the character of the final pieces reflects the fact that all the individual components were made from scratch with a certain look in mind.

Create variations of your theme by experimenting with different shapes and knotting threads.

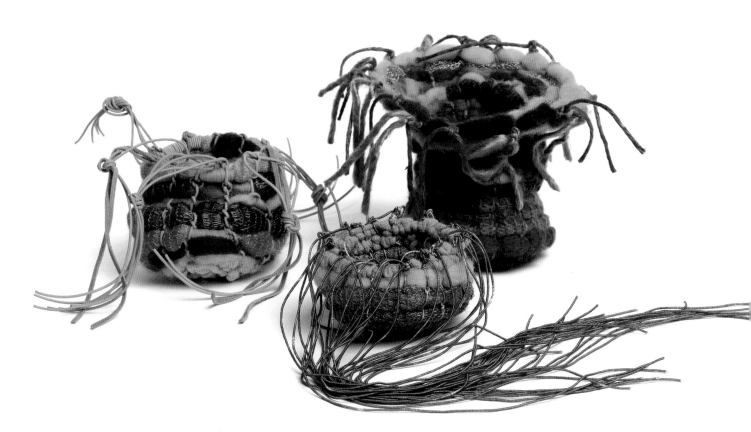

Twined together

Twining involves two or more flexible weavers (the weft element), which are twisted simultaneously around stationary spokes, uprights or a more flexible warp. The weaving elements cross back and forth between the warp elements in a number of different pathways and patterns as explained in this chapter.

Twining across the world

This technique is capable of producing structurally strong forms in many different materials. Examples of the breadth and versatility of this technique can be found in various traditional cultures worldwide, from small-scale pieces of personal apparel, baskets and domestic utensils to body armour and traps.

Specific examples include basket armour from the Pacific coast, Japanese rice-straw sandals, twined wallets and the flexible berry-collecting baskets that are designed to be folded and stored flat. Rigid, lattice structures include fish traps, primitive twined wattle fences and bamboo baskets.

Traditional and modern materials

For the textile artist, this technique can be interpreted in many different ways, whether for large gallery works, small-scale pieces of body adornment or interior pieces. A wide choice of suitable materials for both weavers (weft) and uprights (warp) is available and can offer unlimited potential for creative applications.

The choice of material depends to some extent upon whether a rigid form or a softer, more fluid piece is the aim. For the beginner, it is suggested that initial sampling is worked with relatively rigid warps and flexible weavers both to practise the different twining patterns and to find the most efficient way to hold and manipulate the work. Hand-held methods are outlined on the following pages, other methods include suspending the form when working in the round, as in traditional basket making.

Some examples of suitable materials for the warp stakes include traditional plant forms, such as basket-makers' round- and flat-band ribbon cane, bark strips, sea grass and jute sash-cord. Undyed materials used in chair seating, such as artificial Kraft paper rush, ready twisted natural rush, paper-based cord such as Danish cord and thick cotton cord are all strong and also suitable for twined uprights.

For a completely different look consider using unusual materials, such as clear polythene tubing, nylon polycord, marine rope, electrical flex, strips of metal, leather and suede, wire and fibre knitted tubes (which can be stuffed to make them more rigid if necessary). Machine-stitched cordage stiffened or stitched with wire is another option (see page 17).

Material for the weavers can be equally varied, the only prerequisite being that it is flexible, or can be made so by soaking and mellowing, as you would basketry cane and other hard plant forms. Weavers are generally thinner than the warp material, and need to be strong enough to be twisted in and out of the warps.

Think also how the weft will work in relation to the warp stake. For example, in openwork twining the weavers must be able to grip the warp stakes without sliding up and down. As an example, wire works well against corded paper string or soft textiles, but wire or transparent fishing line twined over polythene tube is more successful for closely packed twining, unless the lines of twining are separated by bead-like objects.

Weavers can be made from any relatively strong textile fibre, such as waxed linen thread, cotton cord, nettle, hemp and jute carpet yarn, weaving and knitting yarns, silk, beading thread including transparent materials, fishing line, elastics and enamelled copper wire and thin steel rope. Fine-cut strips of suede, or leather used in necklace making, can also work well, as can handmade cordage.

Twined vessel, constructed using twisted paper tape and electrical cable hand-dyed with disperse dyes.

The basics of twining

Many different twining sequences and patterns are possible, some of which are illustrated below and can be explored with any number of pliable weavers twined around rigid and flexible warps.

First, some basic twining techniques are sampled in easy-to-handle materials, such as thick paper cord for the passive element, and undyed hemp for the weavers.

The weft (or weavers) consists of two or more ends, which move around groups of warp stakes that are at right angles to the weft. The weavers are the flexible elements, and are used to encircle the stationary warp, twisting around each other and locking the stitch in place.

Note that twining can be constructed flat or in the round, and that working methods include hand-held versions, using a basket makers' screw block (applicable when working with rigid warps) and weighted bobbin twining. This chapter concentrates on hand-held constructions, or twining around hanging shapes.

Remember also that when working in two dimensions the piece is made back and forth across rows. Three-dimensional twining is constructed in rounds, although not necessarily in full rounds, particularly when making free-form and asymmetrically shaped pieces.

Diagram 1: Half twists around single uprights.

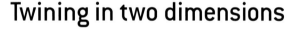

Diagram 2: Half twists around two warps.

Twining in two dimensions

Half-turn experiments

To make a row of half-turn or single-twist twining, use two weavers to encircle every warp stake, alternating the position of the weavers each time one passes behind the warp stake. One element goes behind the spoke, the other in front of it, with a twist in between (see diagrams 1 and 2). A bird's eye pattern results if the two weavers are different colours.

Full-twist experiments

Full-twist twining with one or two warp stakes and two wefts, each of which can be a different colour, is shown in diagrams 3–5. Note that the same colour will always be at the front, and the other to the back of the sample if the pathway described in diagram 3 is followed. Diagram 4 illustrates a variation of this pathway as does diagram 5 in which the wefts alternate between front and back.

Diagram 3: Full twists, double warp.

Diagram 4: Multiple twists, single warps.

Setting out the warp stakes

First lay out a number of stakes parallel to each other on a flat work surface. In this example leave only a small gap, wide enough for the twining element to pass through. A wider space between adjacent warp stakes requires more twists to make a structurally sound piece of work.

For the first row, either temporarily tape the warp stakes to the work surface, use a weight to hold the work firmly in place or hold in the hand.

Diagram 5: Combining single and double warps.

Twining sample. In this piece, the thickness of the weavers is varied to create shape. The sample is worked in cable and craft wire over twisted paper uprights.

Attaching the weavers

To attach the weavers to the warp stakes, select a long weaver and fold it in roughly the proportion of 1:2, so that when the weavers run out, the joins are offset. If you are working with two different colours or materials for the weavers, knot the ends together instead of folding.

Hook the folded weaver over the first warp, which should be held vertically, and bring both ends of the weaver out to the front. Have the long ends going towards the right if you are right-handed, reverse for left. Select the top (or front) weaver and put it behind the next spoke, and back out to the front. Make a half or single twist as described opposite. Follow diagram 1 (opposite) making a series of half twists between each adjacent warp.

The samples can be worked back and forth from left to right and right to left, or turned so that the work is made always from left to right (or vice versa).

Variations

Using the same set-up as described above, experiment with using two warp stakes with single and double twists using two weavers. In diagram 2, opposite, two weavers alternate behind two ribs at a time.

By combining rows of single twists with rows of full twists, or multiple twists on the same sample, the shape will naturally expand and contract in size if the same sized weavers are being used throughout. Another useful method of introducing shape is by varying the thickness of the weavers to introduce shape into a piece (see the sample above). The same principle applies to any combination of patterns that involves more, or fewer, twists.

Alter the appearance of the twining pattern by using a clockwise twist to give an up-to-the-right pattern, or a counter-clockwise twist to give a down-to-the-right pattern. Diagonal stripes are created when the two weavers are of different colours.

Variations can be achieved by twining rows tightly row upon row, or leaving an open warp, or crossing the warp to create a lattice-like effect as shown above.

Lattice patterns

For an easy-to-make version of lattice work, twine every pair of warps together on the first row, for example A plus B, and C plus D. On the next row twine around warp A on its own, then B plus C, and D plus E and so on until the last warp is reached (see diagram 1). Repeat this two-row sequence for as many times as required. For the same effect when twining in rounds, an odd number of warp stakes is needed.

An additional third element is sometimes incorporated into this technique in the form of a horizontal rod or similar. A passive element, it is placed on the surface of the work and twined around by the weavers to incorporate it into the structure.

Decorative elements were traditionally worked with materials too weak to use on their own; this was a common style of single twining in the Pacific North-west of North America. It can be a useful technique for the textile artist to develop, to add richness and variation to contemporary twined work.

Two-dimensional twining in a lattice pattern. Single, double and multiple twists are used here to expand and contract the shape of the sample.

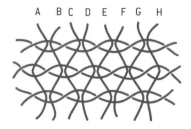

Diagram 1: Pathway of weavers for a lattice pattern.

Moving into three dimensions

Three-dimensional forms can be woven from the top down or bottom up. Working methods outlined on the following pages show how to commence the work in two dimensions, and then how to make the transition between two and three dimensions. There are many ways of doing this, and the interested maker should undertake further study of basketry construction (see Further Reading, page 124).

Although this chapter concentrates on hand-held constructions, an alternative method of twining in the round involves suspending the form on a cord, ideally attached to a swivel (a fishing tackle shop may be able to supply one), which stops the hanging cord twisting around itself.

Two dimensions into three dimensions

Set up a two-dimensional twining sample as described on pages 74–75. Make a few rows of half-twist twining, working back and forth across the horizontal warp stakes, followed by a few rows of full-twist twining. To make the move from two dimensions into three (as shown in the sample below and on page 80), bend the swatch around so the opposite edges come together and twine across the gap between the two edges for several more rounds. To increase the width, add extra twists in the twining, and to decrease make fewer twists. Finish the twined section by going back to twining in rows. Thread the loose ends of the weavers back down alongside a warp stake with a large-eyed bodkin.

Twined form commenced in two dimensions and completed by 'working in the round'.

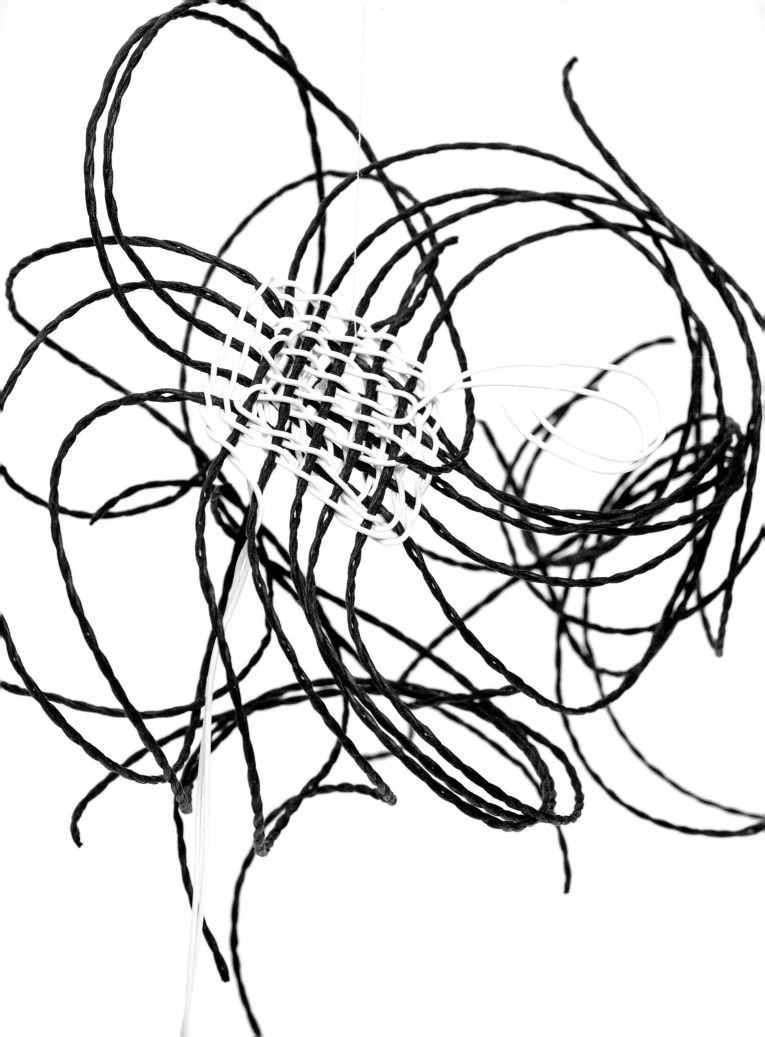

The sample shown opposite was begun with a double square start like the one shown above, in which two twined squares cross each other at right angles.

An experimental twined form using a double square start. The warps are hollow chainette ribbon filled with wire, while the weavers are various weights of gimp.

Double square start

An alternative, easy transition from two to three dimensions can be made using a double square twined start as the base.

To make a similar sample to the one shown opposite, ten identical warps are required, five for each square. In this example thick paper cord was used for the warp and single-core electrical cable with an outer plastic sleeve was used for the weavers. The example shown below was made with tubular chainette yarn, stuffed with thick sisal cord and twined with various weights of gimp. See also the sample on page 23, which illustrates and alternative version in hand-dyed rush and electrical cable using disperse dyes.

Hold five of the warp stakes in the hand and make five rows of horizontal, flat twining at the centre point of these vertical warp stakes. Make two separate squares like the one shown left, leaving the weavers long on one of the pieces. These weavers will be used to twine the two square bases together in the next step (see the sample opposite).

Place one square on top of the other, crossing one another at right angles so that the warp stakes make the shape of a cross. Use the two weavers left hanging from one of the squares, and continue to twine sequentially around each of the four sides of the square.

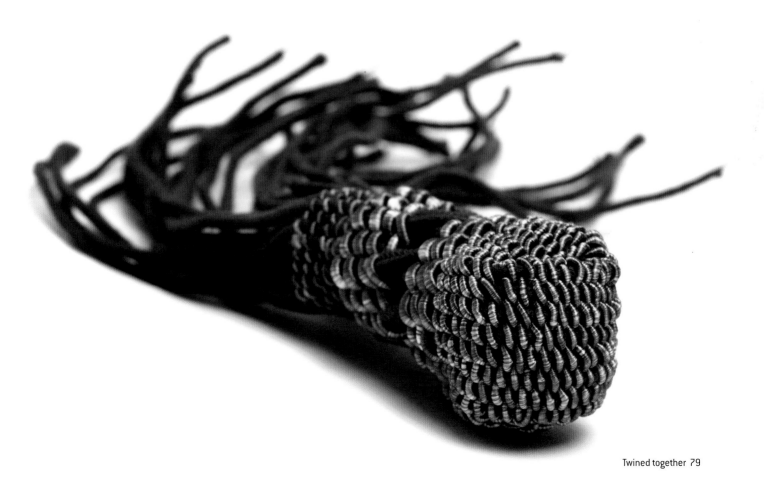

Twine for a few more rounds, gradually manipulating the warp stakes so that they fan out evenly. To move into three dimensions, bend all the warp stakes upwards and grasp them in one hand (or tie together in a bundle at the top to help control the shape). Continue to twine in rounds, taking in all of the warps sequentially.

Use the double square start to make free-form pieces. For example, when working in the round, twine only part-way around, before changing direction, building up an irregular shape as shown in the samples below.

A simple twined form from bottom up

This is a really useful start for pouches and containers, which commences with three rows of flat twining, made at the halfway point horizontally along a group of vertical warp stakes in the same way as you would have made the first row in the sample shown on page 78. The difference here is in the positioning of the first row of twining.

These three rows form the bottom of the pouch (see diagram 1). The next step is to bend all the warp stakes upwards so that the twining can be made in the round, taking in all of the warps sequentially. At this point there will be twice as many warps. Ensure that the weavers are pulled tightly across the gap between front and back warps until the shape of the form is established.

Diagram 1: The start for a twined form worked from the bottom upwards.

The sample on the left demonstrates how to combine two- and three-dimensional twining techniques. The sample on the right is a simple twined form worked from the bottom up.

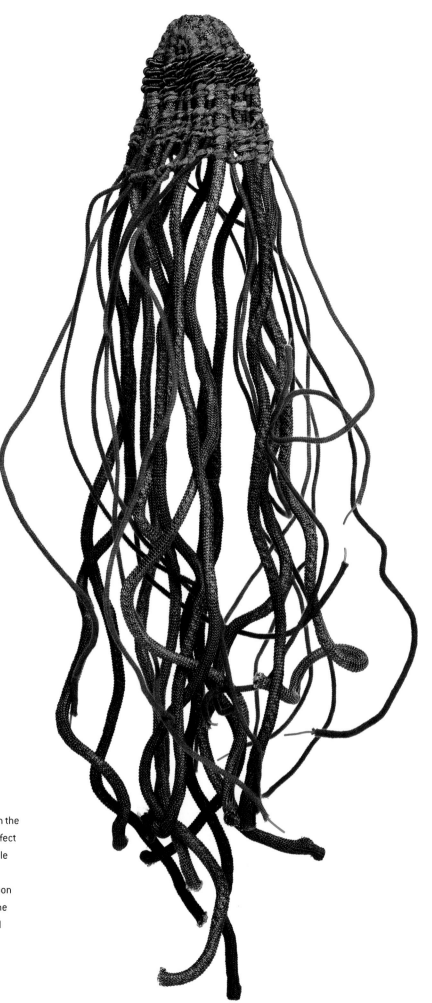

Octopus twined form worked from the bottom upwards. The 'octopus' effect is achieved by hanging the sample upside down. The uprights are constructed from thin hollow ribbon filled with wire and sisal string. The weavers are made from gimp and rayon seam-binding tape.

Experimental twined form worked from the bottom up. The shape is achieved by combining full and partial rounds of twining.

From here on, manipulate the shape, experimenting with various combinations of twining patterns. In the example shown above a tight half-twist twining pattern is used, with just enough space left between each round of twining for the warp stakes to be visible. In this example there are eight warp stakes in hand-dyed tubular viscose chainette filled with sisal string, with the rough side of the knitted tube to the outside. The weavers are viscose seam-binding ribbons, which are gripped relatively securely by the rough texture of the warps.

The paper and wire sample shown opposite is constructed in the same way. The shapes are manipulated by the amount of twists made between weavers, the spaces between each round of twining and the relative tightness of weaving. See the following instructions for more on shaping technique.

Circular bases

Adapted from the world of basketry, the circular base provides a versatile start for rounded forms that can be varied to suit individual projects once the basic principle has been understood and sampled hands-on.

The following instructions can be applied to all manner of suitable materials, and should be adjusted to suit individual preferences. The sample shown opposite is a variation of this technique constructed in thick paper cord and electrical cable.

1. Take six warps, all the same length, and fan out evenly into a circular shape, using a weight (spoke weight, heavy weight from balance scales or ribber weight from a knitting machine) to hold them in place. An alternative working method is to secure them to soft board with a pin for the first round, and then continue to work as directed below.

2. Attach the weavers (as described for the sample shown on page 78) and twine around the spokes once only, beginning approximately 5cm (2in) from the centre point. To do this, fold the weaver and hook over a warp stake to start the process. Once you have completed the first round, remove the weight, and twine for another five rounds, for example.

Beginning of a circular form made from corded paper string twined with electrical cable.

3. Add another six warps (the same length as the first six), one at a time, twining them in place between the existing warps. Continue to twine around all the spokes until the base is a suitable diameter for your purpose.

4. Push the warp stakes in an upward direction to move into three dimensions. An optional next step might be to tie all the spokes together at the top to help form the outline of the three-dimensional shape. Keep this in place for a few rounds of twining.

5. To weave the sides, continue twining until the desired height is reached. Choose to leave open spaces between rounds of twining that can be filled in with decoration, or left open as required. Combine lattice and openwork patterns with bands of close twining, or perhaps introduce a second colour in the weavers to make simple geometric patterns.

6. Neaten the top by pushing the ends of the weavers down alongside the warp stakes on the inside. The warp ends can be made an integral part of the design, as shown in many of the examples in this chapter, or bent over and threaded back on themselves on the inside of the piece. There are many more complex pathways the endings can take, and which can be seen in practice on many twined baskets, both ancient and modern.

Experimental twined forms

Free-form shapes can be constructed by combining flat twining and working in rounds in the same piece. This is particularly effective if the warp stakes are wired as shown here. In the example shown opposite, eight lengths of hand-made cordage were made from 100 per cent cotton chainette tubular yarn, filled with electrical wire approximately 45cm (18in) in length. These are twined with thick gimp thread. Both warp and weft were hand-dyed with direct dyes.

Shaping techniques applicable to both two and three dimensions include adding and removing warps, doubling up the thickness of weavers and combining various twining sequences. Warp stakes can be added or eliminated to achieve the desired shape, a technique that can be further developed to create openwork patterns.

Twined form with double square start (see page 79). The sample combines a closely packed twining pattern with uppermost section worked in a simple lattice pattern.

Small-scale circular starts combined with hand-wrapped cordage (see also page 113).

The samples shown opposite are small-scale versions of circular starts, where the shape is gradually extended and pulled in again as it reaches the top, to make bead-like objects, or endings for hand-wrapped cordage.

Design decisions

Once the basic techniques have been mastered, experiment with negative and positive spaces as design elements. In simple terms this means experimenting with the relative proportions, size and shapes of the gaps and the spaces *in between* the lines made by the warp and weft, as demonstrated in the sample below.

To develop ideas for new shapes based on the samples made thus far, explore ways of working with flexible, easy-to-cut paper, thin card and Tyvek-sheet shapes to make mock-ups. Start by cutting vertical slits into the material to echo the upright warps, bending it and manipulating it in different ways until the overall look of the form is satisfying to the eye. Use a temporary means to hold the form together, such as dress pins or a low-tack adhesive.

Try to analyse why a shape works, recording the details in a personal logbook. Look particularly at the contrast between negative and positive shapes. Reassemble the cut-out shapes, perhaps cutting into them again. Make a photographic record at each of the different stages for future development work.

Two-dimensional twining exploring the possibilities of positive and negative space.

Line, space, line

Inspired by knotted driftwood, cellular structures such as bubbles and microscopic organisms, lacewings and dragonflies, this chapter focuses on knotless netting techniques, which, whether constructed flat or wholly in the round over a former, offer the adventurous textile artist the opportunity to work experimentally with fluid and elastic openwork meshes.

Knotless netting techniques

Examples of ancient netting techniques can be found in practical items such as fishing nets, insect netting and string bags, while modern examples include hairnets, mesh fences and nets used in sporting activities. Historically these nets might have been made between two supporting posts hammered into the ground, or kept taut over the knees or feet.

A simple, yet highly versatile, single-element technique, knotless netting consists of loops that are interlinked and meshed with each other either in rounds, or worked flat in rows. When flat, the dimensions are worked on a straight support cord or rod. It is interesting to note that many of the loops made in knotless netting are similar to the pathways taken by the threads in needle-made lace.

Netting techniques can be inspired by things around us, such as knotted driftwood.

Loop know-how

Sample constructed from nettle yarn. The interconnected loops create different-sized gaps in the net structure.

For the textile artist, knotless netting is a way of making linear patterns in three-dimensional space, constructed from interlinked and interlocked loops. The process is analogous to making drawings with lines, except that here thread and fibres are the chosen medium. To do this successfully, a working knowledge of the main types of loop-stitch is a prerequisite for making loop constructions that work both aesthetically and structurally.

The all-important fact about knotless loop construction is that each loop is interconnected in some way with the loops above and below, and from side to side.

Many variations are possible, once the principle of knotless netting is understood. For example, some loops are made with the yarn entering the head of the previous loop, from front to back or vice versa. Others are interlocked by making a new loop around the head of the loop on the previous row. Or they can be interconnected by simply looping around the bottom of a loop from the previous row, or in a more complex figure-of-eight pathway.

If all the loops have been interconnected correctly the structure should remain in one piece, even if it is designed to have gaps in the netting pattern.

Once the rules have been understood they can be broken. Particular effects, such as the pre-planned disconnected links shown in the sample above, for example.

Netting needles

The netting needle acts like a shuttle and holds a considerable length of yarn (see page 13). However, netting can be made without tools, in which case the yarn will need to be joined at regular intervals. Alternatively the cordage can be plied and twisted from first principles from natural fibres, and joined in as the work progresses. The samples shown here were netted using a needle.

Stitches used in knotless netting

The examples on these pages were netted in two dimensions over holding cords strung up on a frame, as described in Method 1 on page 92.

Interlocking loops

For the initial row, make a series of loops around a rod or holding cord (see diagram 1). For the second row, interlock the new row of loops with the previous row, either netting over and under the bar in between the loops (see diagram 2), or into the loops of the previous row (see diagram 3). The latter will give a tighter stitch.

Knotless netting sample. Various netting stitches, including interlocking and elongated twist stitches were used.

Diagram 1: Row of loops around a holding cord.

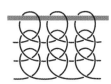

Diagram 2: Second row of loops interlocking with the previous row, under and over the bar.

Diagram 3: Interlocking loops worked into the loops of the previous row.

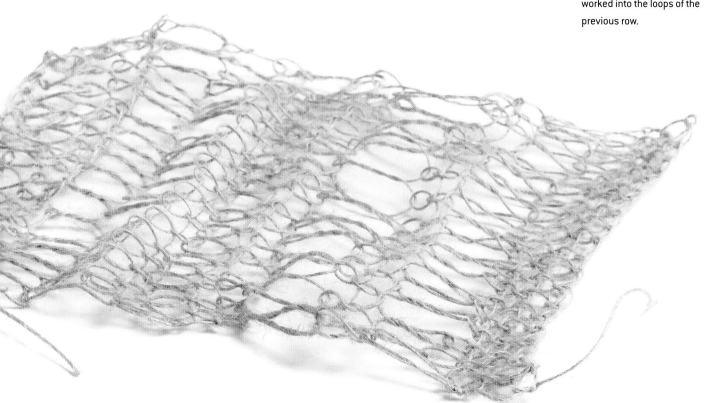

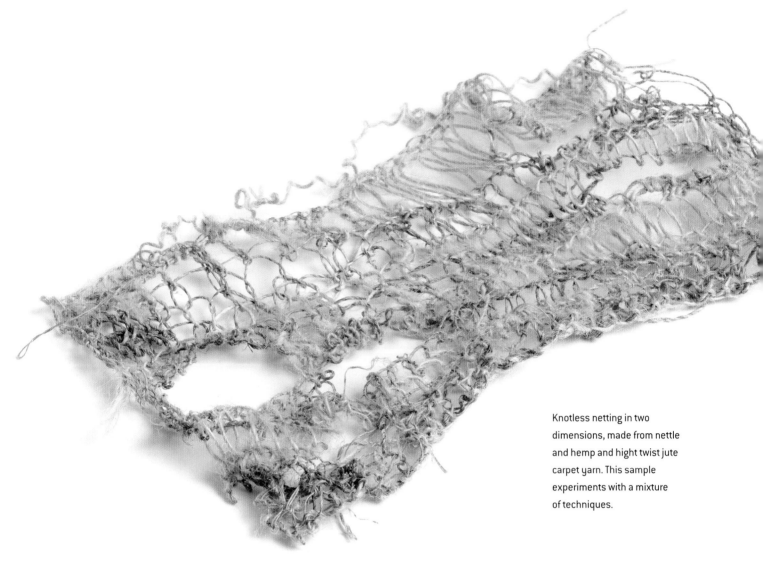

Knotless netting in two dimensions, made from nettle and hemp and hight twist jute carpet yarn. This sample experiments with a mixture of techniques.

Elongated twist stitches

Make a series of loops, as described above for interlocking loops (see diagram 1). To make the twist, continue to work with the same thread, and go back into the loop, twisting it around the loop already made. The more twists there are, the longer the loop. As with the interlocking loops, the next row of elongated twisted stitches can be made by netting into the bar of the previous row of loops, or around the loop itself, for example (see diagram 4).

An alternative method of using a thread and needle to make the twists is to hold the needle down with the thumb of the left hand, while lifting and twisting the under thread with the right hand.

Figure-of-eight loops

This is a variation of twisted loops, but here the pathway of the loop follows the shape of a figure-of-eight. Various loop patterns emerge, depending upon where the loop is interlocked with the previous row of loops. For example, bring the yarn up through the loop of the previous row from the back to the front, then over the front of the lower holding cord, through to the back, and then round the vertical strand of yarn in a figure-of-eight pathway. Repeat for as many loops as required.

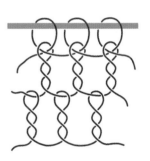

Diagram 4: Elongated twist stitches.

Working in two dimensions

Method 1

This method uses a framework of some sort to make the netting under tension. You could use a rectangular embroidery frame or perhaps a redundant wooden picture frame for small-scale works. This could be seen as a temporary support for use during the making process or as an integral part of a large-scale installation created *in situ*.

In both instances the netting is made over holding cords that can be strung around the frame, roughly parallel to each other or at various angles. Once the netting has been completed the holding cords can be removed (as shown in the samples on pages 90–91), or left *in situ* (as shown opposite).

Using a small frame

Before starting to make the netting, it might be helpful to bind the frame with quilting tape or low-tack masking tape, so that the horizontal holding cords have something to grip to.

To make a similar sample to the one on page 90, choose a strong cotton thread for the holding cords, and wrap it tightly all the way around the frame in roughly parallel lines. These threads are the holding cords over which to make the net.

Work in manageable lengths of yarn, which are threaded up through a large-eyed flat bodkin – ideally use a netting needle, which can hold a substantial amount of thread, and in turn means less joins in the yarn. You could work with waxed linen, strong cotton or high-twist carpet yarn.

Refer to diagram 1 (see page 90) and make a first row of loops as shown, equally spaced along the top of the support thread from left to right. To make this first row stronger, loop around the top and the bottom thread. The subsequent rows were made over the top support thread only.

To make the second row, either work back from right to left, or turn the frame and continue working from left to right, looping over the next row of support thread. When the yarn runs out, splice in a new length.

Make several rows of loops before moving on to creating rows of interlocking loops, loop and twist stitches, elongated twisted stitches and figure-of-eight loops.

Experimenting with mixed techniques

To experiment further with more samples, set up a frame as described above. Make a few rows, keeping each loop the same size. Once a working rhythm has been established, change the pattern of loops, maybe by making two loops into every one loop of the previous row, or extend the loop downwards over two or three lines of support thread. Vary the length of the loop as you progress across the row, to interrupt the regularity of the pattern (see the sample on page 91, for example).

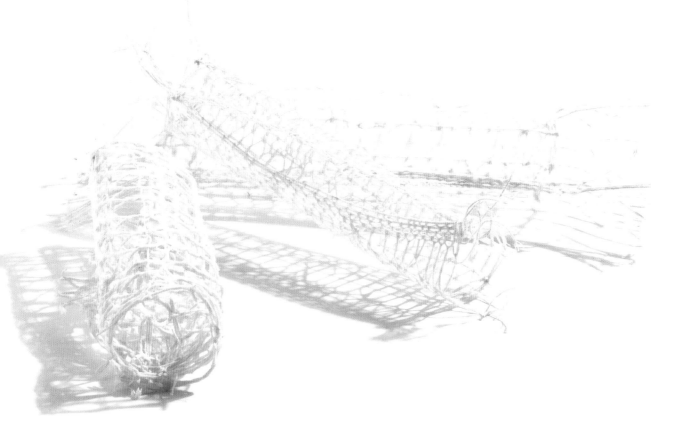

In the samples on this page the support cord is an integral part of the design. To dispense with this element, work over lines of strings as described above, and then cut these holding cords and pull out carefully from the work (see also the sample shown on page 90).

Referring to the sample on page 90 in more detail, note that in some places gaps were created. To recreate this in your own samples, make several interconnected net loops as described above and then skip across selected groups of loops from the previous row without linking into them. Recommence making interconnected loops as before. Repeat across the row as required. Note that even when working free-form it is generally necessary to use a holding cord or rod to commence the netting.

These examples of knotless netting (above) were constructed in two dimensions before being stiffened. The support cord remains an integral part of the design, as shown in this detail (right).

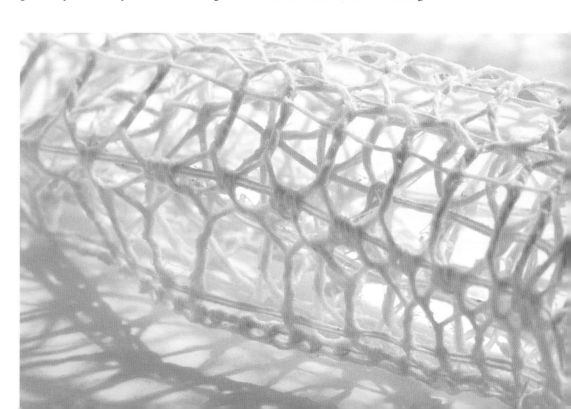

More akin to making a line drawing, beautiful netted structures can be made by eye, tightening and loosening loops to create line and space patterns with a more irregular quality than shown in the previous samples. In the sample opposite, a mix of thick and thin yarns was used to add an extra dimension to the netting pattern. Work using a holding cord, which can be pulled and manipulated to create visual tensions within the piece, or work free-form by eye and without guides as described in method 2, below.

Using more or fewer loops

To alter the width of the netting, add or subtract the number of working loops thus: to decrease the width, net two or more loops together in one action (see diagram 1); and to increase the width, add one or more extra loops into the loop just worked (see diagram 2).

Making changes to the gauge of the netting (i.e. making rows of loops using thinner or thicker fibres) will also increase or decrease the width.

Method 2

This method describes knotless netting worked freely by eye, without the use of a gauge or holding cord to measure the length of the loops. You can think of this method of working as if you were drawing repeating patterns of cell-like linear shapes, where lines of loops are similar yet different in appearance. Netting freehand allows for an anarchic mix of taller and shorter loops, thin and fat loops, and groups of loops that are out of line one with another, rather than made to sit next to each other in any kind of formal pattern.

Choose fibres that are lively and full of character, which will hold a loop pattern open so that the lines of the design are in evidence. You could experiment with springy, lightweight yarns with a tight and irregular twist, such as hand-spun nettle yarn (Crafty Notions) or sisal carpet yarns with a high twist (see also the sample shown on page 89).

Use a piece of dowelling to hold the first row of loops. Secure the dowel to the workbench with G-clamps or duct tape, letting it sit so that the work hangs over the edge of the bench.

Incorporating reclaimed frames

Redundant frames and wire grid structures are an excellent starting point for netting experiments. You could use wooden picture frames, wire and metal meshes, such as old cake-cooling racks and grill-pan grids, or scrap car-engine parts such as gaskets. Alternatives include bent and tied rattan and willow canes that can be tied and lashed together, and frameworks sourced directly from the hedgerow or prunings from trees.

Diagram 1: Decreasing the number of working loops.

Diagram 2: Increasing the number of working loops.

Experiments in three dimensions

Two-dimensional surfaces can be transformed into rigid forms using Paverpol.

One method of constructing three-dimensional samples is to work from two-dimensional shapes, much as you might make an item of clothing from a flat pattern. The second approach is to make three-dimensional forms directly in the round.

Two dimensions into three dimensions

Surface treatments are a great way of working with netting to transform soft textile structures into openwork, rigid three-dimensional forms by using varnishes or hardeners such as Paverpol.

Using Paverpol

Samples can be treated with Paverpol to harden flat pieces of netting (see above and page 93, for example). The netting was manipulated into three-dimensional forms while the Paverpol was drying. To experiment with this method, make a sample net on a framework, as described opposite. Leave the net under tension on the frame, and paint both sides with Paverpol clear hardener, including the support cords if they are to be included in the finished piece. Leave in a warm place to dry, but do not allow it to harden completely.

Manipulate the flat shape into, for example, a tall column as shown on page 93 temporarily tying the open edges together to keep the shape while the Paverpol continues to harden. A temporary former might also be used, but should be made of plastic (or covered in plastic) so that the Paverpol does not adhere to it. Colour can be added to the hardener or painted onto the hardened forms with acrylic colours; a matt glaze can be applied once the fabric hardener is set rock hard.

Note the visual contrast between the treated holding cords, which are stiff and spiky, and the untreated fibres, which make curvilinear shapes spilling over the edges of the forms. Try also crumpling and twisting the stiffened shapes, tying them into place with plastic string until they are completely dry.

Incorporating Tissutex

An additional technique is used in the sample opposite. Layers of torn Tissutex paper have been incorporated into the form to create a second skin. Applied while the Paverpol was drying, the paper and the fibres bonded together to form a single surface. Tissutex is lightweight and yet strong when wet, making it an ideal material for this kind of work.

Using a temporary former or mould

Other methods of working in three dimensions include netting over a temporary former. The sample below shows experiments with layers of nets, contrasting areas of dense, impenetrable netted fibres with more thinly layered areas.

Utilizing the same technique to make flimsy structures more solid, layer over layer can be added in selected areas. Note that the juxtaposition of heavily layered sections with less built-up areas will affect the shape and handle of the finished piece. For example, heavy sections next to thinner areas will affect how a three-dimensional form keeps its shape or folds back on itself (see also the sample on page 98).

Cylindrical form netted over a cardboard tube in carpet yarn and mediumweight undyed gimp.

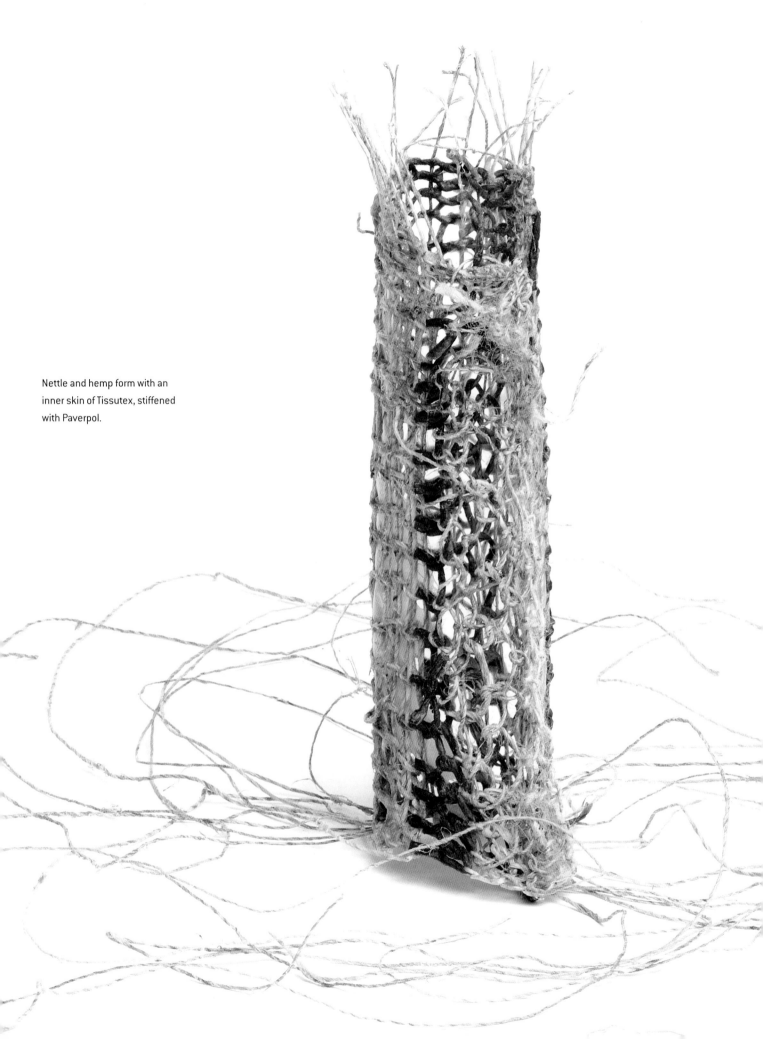

Nettle and hemp form with an
inner skin of Tissutex, stiffened
with Paverpol.

Working in the round

To work in the round with a trial sample, net over a former (cardboard tube, cone or water-pipe insulation material, for example) in the following way. First tie, tape or pin a support cord around the circumference of the former. This can be in the same material as the netting. Leave a long-enough tail end of yarn. Net several rounds first before starting to make horizontal gaps in the net pattern. Refer to the instructions earlier in this chapter (see pages 90–91) and see also the sample shown on page 91.

Using a different fibre, work back over selected areas, rather like making multi-layered darning. If desired, gaps can be made in the next and subsequent layers either to coincide with netted areas of the previous layer, or to make definite holes in the structure (see sample, below). Experiment with larger or smaller loops, or thicker and thinner fibres. Think of the process as if you were building up a drawing from layer upon layer of lines and marks. The sample (opposite) was netted partially over a tubular former and also free form to make the shape wider.

Moving on

To move beyond the obvious technique-led sampling, you need first to learn how to make the loops and net patterns outlined in this chapter. Using this knowledge you can begin to take risks and break the rules to create nets that look like drawings, and drawings that resemble nets, exploiting the netting techniques to create marks and lines in space.

Mix your techniques and materials. The main thing is that the finished piece hangs together as a structurally sound net pattern, where each line is interconnected one to the other using knotless loops.

Multi-layered form netted in biodegradable paper string and nettle yarn.

Make drawings or scans from these pieces as a starting point for other net ideas. Or try some simple exercises to develop design ideas for netting, experimenting with line patterns that focus on the spatial relationships between lines and open spaces using string and masking tape.

Make quick thumbnails or mock-ups, playing with various juxtapositions of loose and tight loops, creating open and closed spaces, adding twists, changing the shape of the nets, working with more or fewer loops than the previous row. Work onto transparent papers to build up dense layers of net patterns.

Take digital photographs, scan the results and manipulate using a simple graphics program, or use the photocopier to make multiple copies to cut up and collage back together, changing the scale, for example, or making negative and positive reversals.

Rework these new net patterns using a combination of fibres and thread. Look particularly at making changes to the scale, and in turn to the context in which the samples might be further developed.

Experiment with assorted materials, including different types of wire, plastic-covered washing line, nylon cords, paper string, waxed linen thread, nettle, hemp and sisal string and thick rope.

Three-dimensional netted 'drawing' in nettle fibres.

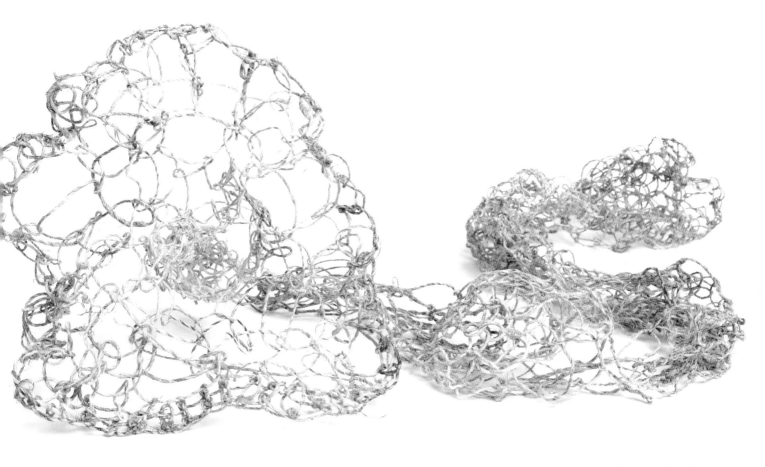

Stringing along

Over the centuries objects have been strung together for decorative, ritual or practical reasons. One example is the packaging technique from rural Japan used for stringing up vegetables and fish to dry on rice straw. Other examples include the strings of garlic, onions and peppers from Europe and South America, and the garlands of flowers offered as greetings to visitors in Hawaii.

Stringing construction techniques

Taking inspiration from these many different cultures, this chapter explores similar construction techniques for stringing objects suitable for use in experimental jewellery projects and as necklace-like, wall-hung pieces.

In this chapter you will find various threading patterns to create hanging strings of lightweight, flat-profile beads, ideas for jewellery and art textiles based on a vertical chaining and chain-looping technique, alongside techniques borrowed from the world of gardening. The properties of different materials are explored for their suitability of purpose alongside their more decorative and aesthetic qualities.

For the textile artist these, mostly functional, stringing techniques offer unlimited potential for experimental and easily made decorative structures, both for wear and for gallery pieces, using repetition, various shaped beads and bead-like objects, changes of scale, texture and colour to create visual interest.

Strings of discs and rectangles

The samples opposite and on page 103 evolved from a series of design ideas initially constructed in card and paper thumbnails (quick sketches), and further developed into strings of printed and painted Tissutex paper and lightweight Lutradur shapes. Strung together with hand-dyed paper yarn to make necklace-like hanging strings of flat discs, squares and rectangles, these experiments would work equally well using flat beads made from metal, wood, glass or plastic, or stiffened fabrics such as organza.

A good starting point for similar pieces would be to mock up design ideas in card or paper. To do this, cut out a series of discs approximately 5cm (2in) in diameter, with a small centre hole of 0.5cm (¼in) diameter. Other holes are offset from the centre, as noted on the following pages. Useful tools for this experiment are a Japanese screw punch for making various-size holes, a compass with cutting attachment to make the discs and a self-heal cutting mat. Gather together a collection of card discs and stringing material, for example a smooth, strong cotton yarn.

Practical tips

A practical tip for stringing lightweight materials is to anchor the work flat on the table with a balance-scales weight, moving the weight along so that it sits on top of the last disc on the string. It is much easier to tie knots and thread the discs when under tension.

When cutting and punching holes through lightweight Lutradur and Tissutex, tape the work to the cutting board and/or use a pad of newspaper between the cutting mat and the Lutradur to give a clean cut through. With care, it is also possible to cut through several layers of Lutradur at the same time. Make sure the blade of the craft knife is sharp, and that you follow all the appropriate safety measures for cutting with, and disposing of, a sharp instrument.

Stringing patterns

The diagrams on the following page offer some ideas for threading sequences, from which you can develop your own designs.

String of overlapping discs constructed from printed Tissutex and hand-dyed Lutradur, strung together with paper tape.

Detailed instructions are given for various stringing patterns, alongside a series of stringing up diagrams. The various stringing cords are shown in different colours so that the pathways can be clearly recognized.

Variations on this threading pattern show how to overlap the discs like a shingle roof or how to separate the discs by the addition of single or multiple knots.

Stringing overlapping discs

1. You will need five discs with centre holes, and two lengths of thread around 60cm (24in) long in contrasting colours (colour A and B) so that you can see the pathway of the stitches. Find the middle of the threads and double over, giving four ends each 30cm (12in) in length.

2. Mount these threads together through the centre hole of the first disc, using a lark's head (reversed double half hitch) knot (see page 33). Let the threading strings hang downwards. Work first with colour A until all the discs have been strung, then with colour B (see diagram 1).

3. Working on a flat surface, take the next disc to be strung and thread colour A through the centre hole from the front to back. Colour B will strand across the back of the disc. Take the next disc to be strung, and thread colour A through the centre hole from the back through to the front. Colour B will continue to strand across the back of the work. Thread up all five discs in this manner.

4. Go back to the top of the string, and string colour B as follows. Thread through the centre hole from the back through to the front of the second disc, and from front to back on the third disc. Repeat this procedure for as many times as required, as shown in diagram 1.

5. Note that the discs can be pushed up the string, overlapping the bottom half of one disc with top half of the next disc. Arrange the way the discs overlap as desired and draw up the string cord so that it fits snugly against the final disc in the string. Knot the stringing cords together to secure the threaded-up discs.

Note: When threading up long strings of beads, it is easier to work with both threads one after the other on every pair of discs, rather than stringing up the whole length with one colour after the other. Use flat bodkins or a large-eyed sewing needle to assist with threading. A spot of clear nail polish or Fray Check will stop the ends of the stringing material shredding during the stringing process.

Stringing discs with separations

In these examples one or more knots are used to lock individual discs into position so that they are separated from each other (see diagram 2).

1. Cut two lengths of thread around 60cm (24in) long for every five discs in contrasting colours (colour A and B) so that you can see the pathway of the stitches. Find the middle of the threads and double over, giving four ends each 30cm (12in) in length.

2. Mount these threads together through the centre hole of the first disc, using a lark's head (reversed double half hitch) knot (see page 33).

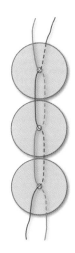

Diagram 1: Threading pattern for stringing overlapping discs.

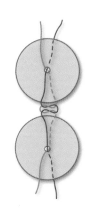

Diagram 2: Knots can be used to separate discs.

Printed and hand-dyed
Lutradur and Tissutex discs.
Each disc has been decorated
with plastic buttons and strung
together with nettle fibres.

3. Take the next disc to be strung and thread colour A through the centre hole from the front to back. Colour B will strand across the back of the disc. Thread colour B up through the same centre hole, from the back through to the front of the disc.

4. Tie a single overhand knot using colour A and colour B as in the sample shown below.

5. Repeat steps 3 and 4 as many times as required.

Overlapping discs with pairs of holes

Discs of 5cm (2in) diameter each with pairs of holes situated approximately 1cm (¼in) from opposite edges can be strung so that the top and bottom 1cm (¼in) of each disc are overlapped.

Thread the discs together using the threading sequence in diagram 3 as your guide. Thread colour A from front to back through the first hole. Colour B will strand across the back of the disc. Thread colour B up through the same centre hole from the back through to the front of the disc. Colour A will strand across the back of the disc. Finally, thread colour A from back to front through the second hole. Colour B will strand across the back of the disc. The second disc is threaded in the same way: continue the threading pattern using colour A to make the link between the two discs on the front side.

Using the same principle as shown in diagram 2 on page 102, these two-holed discs can also be separated from each other by knots.

Diagram 3: Discs strung with pairs of holes.

String of printed and dyed Lutradur and Tissutex discs. Each disc is divided from the next with an overhand knot.

Stringing rectangles with two equidistant holes

In this example rectangles are strung together, developing the threading patterns already covered in the previous diagrams. String along both edges or along one edge only. Use simple overhand knots to separate individual units, if desired. Explore other, more complex knotting patterns to space out the discs, referring to chapter 3 for further inspiration.

Two-colour stitching technique

Diagram 4 (right) shows the stitch pathway for linking two edges together, to join flat rectangles into three-dimensional cylindrical shapes, for example.

Making and stringing three-dimensional Lutradur beads

Constructed in short strings of three or four units using the techniques described above, simple lightweight, three-dimensional beads can be made by knotting the beginning of the chain of rectangles to the end of the chain.

These individual units can then be strung together using punched holes and two ends of stringing material in the same manner as described above for two-dimensional discs.

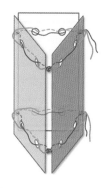

Diagram 4: Three-dimensional threading pattern.

Lutradur beads strung together with nettle yarn.

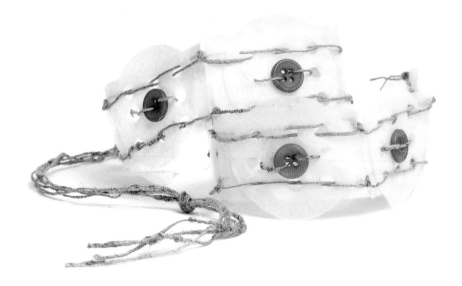

String things

The samples above and below illustrate string things inspired by Japanese packaging techniques, as reflected by the choice of materials and the less-is-more approach. The multi-layered units in these samples were individually assembled before being strung together.

The sample shown opposite is constructed from five spiky ball shapes, which were strung together with two ends of plastic-covered electrical wire.

To make the balls you will need separate lengths of ruched cordage made from undyed tubular cotton chainette yarn filled with a length of wire and a layer of the chainette yarn using the Fasturn system (as described on pages 11 and 18–19). Tie short lengths of hemp yarn along the ruched tubes and hand-roll the latter into balls.

Find the centre of the stringing wire and bend it back, so that you have two working ends. Push end A through the centre of a ball and allow end B to travel on the outside to rejoin A as it emerges from the centre of the ball. Tie a series of knots to space the balls before repeating the process as many times as required.

Multi-layered Lutradur discs and rectangles, strung together with nettle yarn and decorated with buttons.

Layered Lutradur rectangles strung together with nettle yarn.

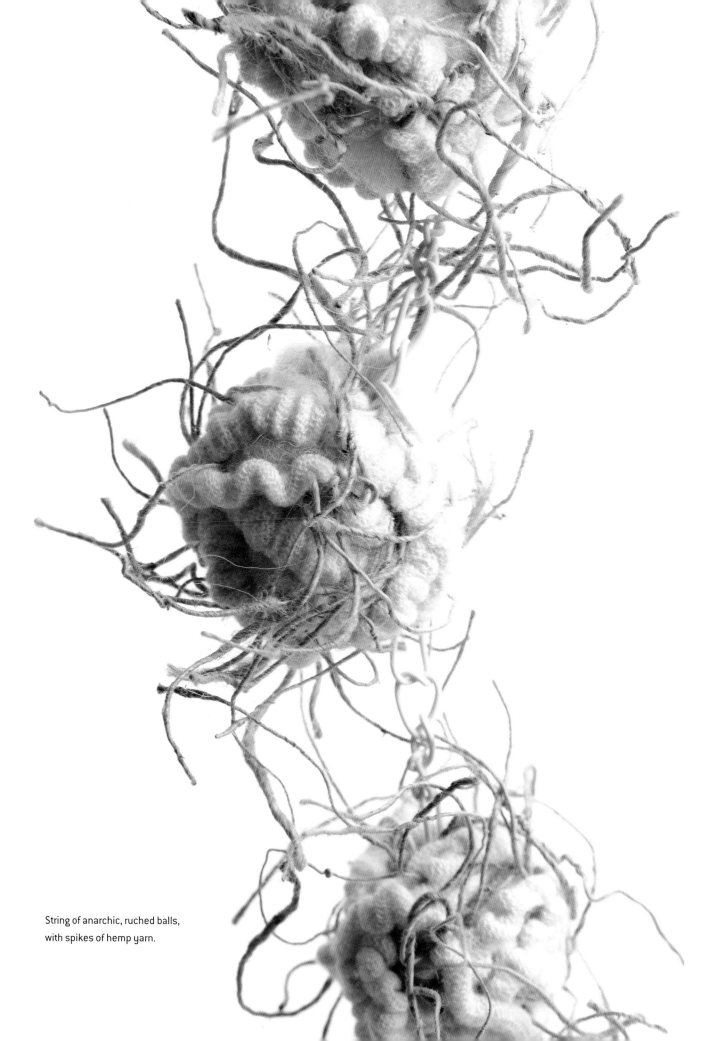

String of anarchic, ruched balls,
with spikes of hemp yarn.

Printed and perforated cylinders strung together with hand-dyed waxed linen thread.

In the sample shown above the stringing material (hand-dyed, waxed linen thread) encircled the perforated tubes before being rejoined and twisted together to separate the cylinders. Note also that the stringing cords were threaded through the line of stitching that joins the cylinders together to hold them in place.

Chaining techniques

Chain loops

Method 1
Practise making a chain of interlinked loops using your hand instead of a crochet hook. Work with thick cotton cord, or work with several ends of thinner yarn. The process is very similar to chaining-off a warp from the warping board with your hands – a loop is made in the end of the warp, the warp is drawn through the loop, and the process repeated, pulling and pushing the loops to tighten them up.

Repeat the sequence, pulling the third loop through the second loop and so on. To use this technique to develop ideas for string things, every so often open out a loop and insert (for example) a length of ruched cordage into it, pulling the loop tightly around the cord to hold it in place. This technique works best with textured objects that will not slip out of the loop.

The sample shown opposite develops the chain-loop technique further. Here single loops are made in a length of doubled-over, handmade cordage at widely spaced intervals. The insertions were made from lengths of ruched cordage, which were wrapped and bound together (see chapter 4) before being contained within the loops. The cordage is twisted and bound with a figure-of-eight wrap in hand-dyed and printed wool fabric.

Experimental string of
chain-looped insertions
made from ruched cordage.

Method 2

Tie the cord around your finger or thumb to make a loop on the right hand
(or vice versa if you are left handed).

Wrap the working end of the cord under and over your finger to form a second loop.
Pull the first loop over the newly formed loop, dropping it off so that only one loop
remains on your finger. Use the other hand to tension the cord, pulling downwards
and upwards on the new loop to tighten it. Repeat the process.

Method 3

Make a slipknot loop, leaving a long tail of cord. Hold the loop open over the middle
finger and thumb of your right hand. Tension the working yarn in the left hand as you
would for crochet, feeding the cord over the raised middle finger. Pinch the short end
of the cord in such a way that the fingers of the right hand can grasp the working end
of cord to make a loop, drawing it through the existing loop on your right hand.

To control the flow of the cord, raise and lower the middle finger (like a scissors
action) as the new loop is being formed and drawn through the old loop.

Move the forefinger and thumb of the left hand close to the loop you have just
made, pulling downwards as you raise the middle finger before making the next
loop. Continue in this manner to make a continuous chain of loops.

Chain loops with beads

Develop ways of inserting bead-like objects into the chains as you work. For example,
at every fourth chain take the loop off the finger, or the hook, and poke the loop
through the opening in a ring or washer, for example.

Replace the loop onto the hook or finger and continue to make chain loops until
you want to incorporate the next ring or washer.

Vertical chaining techniques

Stringing Japanese style

Traditional Japanese packaging can be both functional and beautifully simple in design, making use of readily available natural materials. These methods, traditionally used for stringing up vegetables and fish to dry onto lengths of rice straw cord are a beautifully simple way to chain, twine and tie similar-shaped objects together.

Seen as a starting point to inspire small-scale decorative projects such as bracelets and accessories, the sample below shows lengths of hand-painted, rolled-paper cord bound together with hand-dyed paper string, and twisted cords made from embroidery silks chained together.

Neckpiece or bracelet constructed using vertical chaining techniques. Hand-painted and twisted paper string is twined with commercially dyed embroidery threads. The embroidery threads were plied together to make a cord twister.

To construct a similar sample, assemble several lengths of rolled paper cord measuring approximately 6cm (2½in) in length, and two long lengths of suitable cordage, for example paper string or gimp.

Find the middle of the two lengths of cordage, double over and mount together over the first length of rolled paper using a lark's head (reversed double half hitch) knot (see page 33).

Lift up a pair of cords from cordage A and lay the next length of rolled paper parallel to the first length of rolled paper cord, so that it sits over the remaining pair of cords from cordage B (see diagram 1).

Separate the upper pair of cords so that you can bring the bottom pair of cords up between them, as shown in diagram 1.

The bottom cords are now uppermost and the upper cords become the lower pair (see diagram 2). Place the next length of rolled paper between the upper and lower pairs of cords.

Repeat the process as described above until all the lengths of rolled papers have been twined together (see diagram 3).

The samples opposite and on the following page show examples of vertical chaining in a variety of fibres suited for experimental jewellery projects.

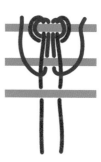

Diagram 1: Mounting two lengths of cordage.

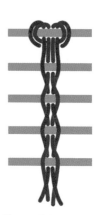

Diagram 2: Bottom layer of cords are now uppermost.

Diagram 3: The completed chaining sequence.

Two examples of the vertical chaining technique. The left-hand sample is constructed from commercially dyed, ruched cordage twisted with wire. The other is made from bias tape and handmade wrapped cordage.

Stringing objects onion style

Onions, peppers and garlic are traditionally strung onto strong string, or plaited together for winter storage in Europe. In South America, *rista* is the practice of stringing or threading brightly coloured peppers, garlic and onions for storage and presentation or decoration.

Onions are usually strung while the stems are still pliable. Each onion stem is woven into a holding string, one on top of the other. The weight of each new onion locks the previous onion in place. The string is hung up while the work is carried out.

To simulate the process using textiles, remember that this is a simple under-over weaving in process, where the doubled holding string is the warp, and the ruched cordage or 'onion stems' form the weft. Refer to page 56 for an example of this technique in practice. Here is how to make a practice sample:

1. Take a long length of strong cord. Double it over and tie a knot in the loose ends to fasten them together and to make a loop. Hang from a hook on the back of a door, or secure with a G-clamp to the workbench.

2. Start the process at the bottom of the string by making a chain loop, as described on page 108. Insert the first ruched cord into the loop and draw the loop up tightly. The weight and the texture of the cord should hold it in place.

3. Add the next ruched cord by separating the string into two ends. This is the warp or passive element. Use the cordage as weft, weaving it around the warp strings in an under-and-over sequence for three rows or more.

4. Make sure that the ruched cord is pushed tightly against the string in a downward movement before stringing up the next piece.

5. String up as many objects as needed. Weave cords in alternately from the left and the right.

Daisy chains and much more

Inspired by daisy chains, the piece shown on page 17, for example, is made up of two units of slitted stems and top knots, which combine wrapping, twining and knotting techniques constructed from machine-stitched cordage.

Traditional daisy chains are made with freshly picked daisies. Slits are made in the stems of the daisy. Poke the stem of one daisy through the slit made in the stem of a second daisy. The slit must be small enough so that the flower head cannot pull back through the slit. Keep repeating this process until the desired length of chain is reached. The chain can be joined to make a complete ring.

To replicate in textiles and fibres, use wrapping and binding techniques to make the slits. You will need a core made up of at least two elements. Work either from the topknot down or the bottom up, depending upon the design and the techniques used.

Working from the bottom upwards make a length of wrapped fibres, leaving long tails hanging loose for added decoration at the start of the stem. To make the slit, divide the core into two separate elements and wrap each section individually for the length of the slit. Rejoin the core elements and wrap as one until the topknot or 'flower-head' section is reached.

Work a crown knot or similar to complete the unit. Make several units in this manner and link together, pushing the topknots through the gaps in the 'stems'.

Use twining techniques to create a circular start (see page 86) and then wrap the cores back together to complete an attractive top knot.

Working from the topknot down, first make a spherical bead-like knot using twining techniques (see page 86). Wrap all the bundle core threads together, sub-dividing for the slit and rejoining to make a solid stem.

Complete this unit with a small, twined cup shape. Separate the bundle of core threads out so that they become the passive elements. Add new threads for the active twining cords.

Three dimensions into two dimensions

The goal of the creative textile artist should be to combine textile techniques in the same way that marks and lines are combined in drawing. To feel confident, and to be in control of these many different ways of working, can take years of practice.

Individual approaches

If you hone and refine these practical skills, the ability to translate visual research, or develop a concept from first principles, will become second nature. This final chapter suggests a variety of individual approaches that readers might take as a starting point for their own personal creative journey.

The ability to move between thinking and working in two and three dimensions, and using assorted techniques and materials, means that for the textile artist, making becomes as natural as writing or speaking.

Three-dimensional radial coiling technique using newspaper and string.

Pages from the author's sketchbook showing patterns in the landscape.

It is here that using a digital camera and computer imaging can help. Thumbnail sketches can be developed quickly by taking images of the three-dimensional constructions back to the drawing board for further work. Changes to scale, colour, shape and form can all be visualised, refined or further improved in function or concept, or perhaps rejected.

Similarly, by the use of more traditional technologies, images of three-dimensional artwork can be transformed into two-dimensional prints using block-print processes, or more sophisticated methods such as screen-printing using photographic techniques.

This chapter addresses these issues, and suggests ways forward so that the reader is able to develop his or her own visual language. Having explored many of the techniques outlined in this book, the next step is about developing these initial explorations into something more tangible; for example a decorative item or, for interior applications, a piece of textile art or a gallery installation constructed *in situ*.

Working from first principles, this chapter demonstrates links between textile samples and inspiration derived from linear patterns in the landscape and in microscopic organisms. It is here that technique is seen as a way of interpreting the source, rather than an exercise in a particular technique. Some simple studio exercises are suggested to complement the making process.

Pattern in the landscape

Inspiration for this chapter is from the author's own work. Three-dimensional works constructed in newspaper, paper tape and paper string, exploring radial coiling as a way of making spiral shapes, form one starting point for this creative journey (see sample opposite). Originally these experiments were intended as mock-ups for large-scale works for an exterior environment.

Another source of inspiration came from a series of two-dimensional landscape drawings made at a later date. These illustrations (above) show pages from the author's sketchbook of patterns in the landscape using rubbings from small-scale pieces of natural material, such as weathered driftwood and shells. These reflect larger scale linear patterns found in the Yorkshire Dales landscapes.

Colour studies derived from bubbling, spiralling mud pools (see page 27) add yet another dimension, as does a series of small twined forms constructed in paper yarn, and over-dyed electrical cable.

Connections between different bodies of work are not always particularly obvious if the works were made over a long period of time.

Reviewing and refining work, both in the long and short term, is a natural part of the creative process, and should be seen as pointing to the next stage in an individual artist's development. Links are sometimes made simply by random juxtapositions of old and new works pinned up on a studio wall, or perhaps a visit from a fellow practitioner, who will see the work with a fresh eye.

Experimental swirling spiral form constructed with wrapping and binding techniques. The sample is made from linen yarn over a cotton core and has been piece dyed using direct dyes.

Spiral combined with free-form swirls. These coils of paper yarn are painted with reactive dyes.

Closed and open experimental form made from linen yarn wrapped over a cotton cord. This sample has been piece dyed with direct dyes.

The landscape drawings were the starting point for two-dimensional textile prints, but when placed next to the previously made coiled forms, the visual links became much clearer, particularly in the use of line, the recurring spiral shapes and the idea of taking the inside outside. The moody colours and spiralling forms from the colour notebook also have a similar linear quality, reflecting more colour-stories derived from the landscape of the Yorkshire Dales.

This final chapter shows a little of the thinking behind a new creative journey, where particular elements are selected from these previous works, cross-referenced and further refined into potential new pieces in two and three dimensions.

Drawing with thread.
Free-machine stitching
inspired by pattern in
the landscape.

Working from first principles

To begin the creative journey, some ideas for studio exercises inspired by linear patterns in the landscape, working initially in two dimensions, are outlined below. The hardest part, as always, is getting started and overcoming the fear of the blank white sheet of paper.

A selection of quick practical experiments are suggested as warm-up exercises. They can be used as starting points for textile construction techniques, from primary sources of reference such as patterns in the landscape. At the same time the reader is encouraged to sketch, draw and collage in a personal journal, working back and forth between making with fibres, and recording and developing ideas through drawing.

Explore working with non-traditional methods, some of which are outlined below. Look particularly at experimenting with digital technology, if it is available to you, as a tool for developing design ideas.

Experimental doodles with a purpose

Doodling with a purpose, using string or thick rope wrapped with masking tape, is a quick and easy way to visualise designs. Double over a long length of string and pull up sections to make a series of loops, binding the two ends of string together to emphasize the looped sections, rather as if you were doing joined-up handwriting.

Add in extra sections of string, branching out to make new lines of loops and wraps. Change the scale by selecting thicker and thinner strings and ropes, making the bound and wrapped sections wider and narrower so that the string lines sit closer together, or so that there is more space between the loops.

Carry out a series of experiments using this method. Scan the results, or make photocopies, layering one over the other in different permutations to suggest design ideas that can be taken back into practical wrapping experiments, or turn them into simple block prints, as described below.

Drawing lines with threads

Lines can be thick, thin, textured, smooth, rough and drawn with pen and ink, brush and watercolour, various grades of pencil, chalk, pastel or emulsion paint. Try to find an analogy in thread and fibres, perhaps using a series of descriptive words to sum up the character of the handmade cordage, for example.

Just as lines and marks in studio design work are the building blocks for more complex image-making, the same concept applies to using handmade cordage to construct surfaces and forms from first principles. This is about taking ownership of the whole design process rather than always using off-the-shelf yarns and fibres.

Instead of drawing or painting a variety of lines, make a series of knotted or wrapped strings and experimental cordage inspired by the drawn lines shown on page 115. Select one of these experiments, repeating it in horizontal or vertical stripes, to build up various textured surfaces. Use print, scans or photocopies to make quick thumbnail images before moving on to constructing more complex patterns in fibres.

Think of the process of making experimental cordage as drawing lines with thread. The character of a hand-rendered line varies considerably depending upon your chosen drawing media, speed of making the mark on the paper and the pressure you use to draw with. Apply this thinking to the chains of knots, wrappings and binding made with lines of thread and the like.

Exploring line and space with wrapped paper cord.

Screen-printed Lutradur (left) and experimental screen prints (right) derived from patterns in the landscape.

Prints developed from knot and net patterns

Looking like half-written lines of text, some of the knot and net patterns illustrated in chapters 3 and 7 could be developed further as textile pieces in their own right, or used as a jumping-off point for making relief textures on simple printing blocks.

To make a relief-print block, glue a chain of knots onto a baseboard with PVA or a similar waterproof medium. Allow time for the PVA to dry out thoroughly. Roll up the surface with a suitable printing ink (emulsion-based ink, for example) and print the resulting pattern as a single image, or in repeat onto a variety of surfaces.

Consider taking the prints one step further by working back into them with various different fibres and thread, to raise the surface and emphasize underlying rhythms and patterns in the design.

Combining techniques

As you become fluent in the various techniques, aim to translate the lines and marks you have made on paper into knotted, wrapped, bound or looped lines, where you become aware only of the expressive quality of marks and lines the threads form.

In the same way that you might make raised surfaces and collages with card, paper and paints from a primary source of inspiration, the same principles can be applied to fibre and textile experiments in two and three dimensions.

Substitute card and paper for heavy-duty canvas, sackcloth, scrim, thin muslin, cotton, open-mesh canvas, felted wool, or non-woven surfaces such as Tyvek, Lutradur, types of non-adhesive interfacing and lightweight garden fleece for example. Three-dimensional forms can be built up over an armature of plastic and wire meshes.

Frames and apertures

The working surface needs to be made taut. A temporary solution is to use an embroidery hoop or rug-making frame to stretch the base to make it firm while working into it. Alternatively, incorporate a framework into the piece as an integral feature of the design. Use temporary or permanent fabric stabilizers to make fragile and thin surfaces more workable.

Thread cords back and forth through the surfaces with a bodkin. Consider also making a series of punched or cut apertures into the working surface, outlining the pattern for example, or work directly into open weaves and wire or plastic meshes.

Various methods for making holes include machine-stitched buttonholes and eyelets opened up with a stiletto point, and insertion of sail-makers' grommets, or other types of eyelets (corset-making suppliers might be useful here). As shown in chapter 8, a bookbinding screw punch works well on a variety of surfaces.

A third solution is to use a warped-up wooden frame as described in chapter 7 (see page 94) for knotless netting experiments. This technique is suitable for wrapping and knotting experiments (see below).

Experimental drawing with fibres

Try this simple experiment. Use a flat bodkin or similar to make lines of knots over a prepared base, as described above, linked to the base at regular intervals to create knotted drawings. Combine surface knotting with wrapping techniques, experimenting with a wide variety of materials with differing properties, such as Tyvek fabric, heavy-duty Lutradur and openwork scrim. Try different weights of fibres on these surfaces, noting how they react with the base.

Continue working in the same manner using wrapping and binding techniques (see chapter 4). To wrap onto an existing surface, first attach bundles of core threads to the working surface, as described below.

Pull a length of thread, or threads, up through the surface from the back to the front. Make a stitch the length of the section that will be wrapped, ending with the thread at the back of the work. Do this several times so that there are parallel rows of threads, one next to the other. Draw the thread to the front of the work and commence wrapping around and around this bundle of threads.

Explore ways of subdividing the bundle of threads, regrouping them and using different yarns as the wrapping elements. Make the long stitches (core fibre) a different length to the taut surface. A longer length of wrapped cordage will stand proud of the surface, whereas shorter wrapping will encourage the surface underneath to wrinkle and pucker. To experiment with short wrappings, you'll find it easier to remove the work from the hoop or frame.

Taking it further

Warp up a suitable frame with even or random spacing, combining thick and thin fibres for added interest. Search out found objects, both as a framework and to move the work into three dimensions.

Wrap, knot, bind, twist and loop threads around the stationary warps, referring to source drawings and photographs for inspiration. Concentrate on translating the essence of these images into textile structures, using three-dimensional textile techniques as a tool, as you would with any other traditional drawing equipment.

Use the warp stake, singly, as pairs and other groupings to create branch-like structures, binding one to the other and then sub-dividing them in different ways. Combine hand-wrapped windings with bindings, using the overhand or half-hitch knot, or build layers of warp-wrapped surfaces one over the other to form complex structures in two and three dimensions.

Blending old and new technologies

With the advent of digital technology it is possible to move easily between two dimensions and three dimensions, and between hands-on and virtual image making. The main downside of all off-loom techniques such as those described above is that they are nearly all relatively slow processes.

To move on as a textile artist, finding ways of developing design ideas quickly is a paramount concern. It is here that digital solutions might be considered a way forward. Keeping a digital sketchbook to supplement traditional hands-on practice (for which I believe there is no substitute) is a useful method.

A three-headed form bringing together influences from two-dimensional imagery and experimental three-dimensional forms. The piece is knotted and coiled in gimp and seam binding tape, and covered with millinery wire. It is piece dyed with direct dyes. See a close-up detail on page 45.

For example, you could take digital photographs of three-dimensional structures or scan two-dimensional samples directly to the computer. Manipulate the latter digitally to create virtual three-dimensional repeat patterns derived from hands-on samples. Alternatively, make a series of printouts that can be photocopied several times over, and in different scales, to make mock-ups of the proposed designs. This is a useful working method for observing how a single-unit, three-dimensional sample of, say, knotting would look if repeated many times over.

Changes of scale, distortion of the image, experimenting with negative and positive versions of the image, and different colourways can all be visualized much more quickly than with hands-on making. Work back and forth between digital and hands-on practice, going on to develop those images that have the most potential for development into resolved projects.

Other options include making two-dimensional digital textile prints from the scanned and manipulated constructions, which might be further embellished with stitch, or worked into again with any suitable off-loom techniques.

One thing leads to another

Take digital photos of small-scale samples and/or scan samples direct into the computer (scanners can cope well with lumpy or uneven surfaces). Manipulate these images on your computer: for example, multiply, change the scale and colour, build mock-ups of virtual pieces. This can be an effective and quick way of developing designs with these normally very time-consuming techniques. Working from these images, the next step is to move back into making or developing ideas through drawing.

Moving on

It can be argued that contemporary fibre artists, while incorporating the wisdom and knowledge of their predecessors, have taken traditional textile construction techniques beyond the functional and turned them into an art form that is not just an imitation of past work, but also something fresh and individual.

To move on and develop a personal handwriting in three-dimensional textile construction techniques, look to what others are doing in this very broad field of creative work. Compare and contrast traditional usage of off-loom techniques with current working practice employed by contemporary fibre artists, in particular how traditional materials are used in a contemporary context, or the interpretation of these ancient techniques in modern and unexpected materials.

There is much in the way of reference material available from museum artefacts, gallery shows and contemporary publications. The internet has also given us a really valuable research tool, but there is still no substitute for seeing real works and responding to the tactile sensibility of the maker, and the context in which it was made, whether those artefacts are ancient or modern.

Further reading

Butcher, Mary, *Contemporary International Basketmaking* (Merrell Publishers, 1999)

Edmonds, Janet, *Three-Dimensional Embroidery* (Batsford, 2009)

Emery, Irene, *The Primary Structures of Fabrics: An Illustrated Classification* (Thames and Hudson, 2009)

Issett, Ruth, *Colour on Cloth* (Batsford, 2009)

Itten, Johannes, *The Elements of Colour* (John Wiley & Sons, 1970)

Lark Books (editors), *500 baskets: A Celebration of the Basketmakers Art* (Lark Books, 2006)

Lee, Ruth, *Contemporary Knitting for Textile Artist* (Batsford, 2007)

Rossbach, Ed, *Baskets as Textile Art* (Van Nost. Reinhold, 1979)

Rossbach, Ross, *The Nature of Basketry* (Schiffer Publishing, 2004)

Wilcox, Michael, *Blue and Yellow Don't Make Green* (School of Color Publishing, 2002)

Suppliers

Texere Yarns
College Mill
Barkerend Road
Bradford
West Yorkshire
BD1 4AU
Tel: 01274 722191
Fax: 01274 393500
www.texere-yarns.co.uk
email: info@texere.co.uk
Suppliers of white linen and natural pure linen, high twist pure cotton, cotton ribbon, hollow chainette cotton ribbon yarn, 100% cotton, recycled cotton cord, strong undyed recycled cotton yarn, spun silk, Texere Picasso gimp (medium and heavyweight types available), Pinewood viscose ribbon (4-ply, DK and super chunky), jute, natural raffia, leather thonging, dyed merino wool tops.

Anna Crutchley
Email: acrutchley@braidsociety.com
Offers a range of equipment and supplies for making cords and tassels, including the Anna Crutchley cordtwister for making 2, 3 and 4 strand cords and rope.

Spunart
1 Park Lane
Allestree
Derby
DE22 2DR
Tel: 01332 554610
www.spunart.co.uk
Email: sales@spunart.co.uk
Suppliers of Lutradur fabric, an ideal medium for textile art.

The Color Wheel Company
P.O. Box 130
Philomath
OR 97370-0130
E-mail: info@colorwheelco.com
www.colorwheelco.com
Suppliers of colour wheels and colour theory resources.

Kemtex Educational Supplies
Chorley Business & Technology
Centre
Euxton Lane
Chorley
Lancashire
PR7 6TE
Tel: 01257 230220
Fax: 01257 230225
www.kemtex.co.uk
Products supplied include Procion, Disperse, Direct, Acid and Indigo Dyes. Also supplies associated chemicals for dyeing and information sheets on dyeing and safety data.

Michael Williams
Tel: 0114 2721039
Email: wood@sewilliams.me.uk
www.michael-williams-wood.co.uk
Good quality, hand-made wooden articles for textile crafts made to order, including couronne sticks.

The Crazy Wire Company
Unit 2
Back Avondale Road
Morecambe
LA1 1SW
Tel: 01524 417700
www.wireandstuff.co.uk
Email: crazywirecompany@aol.com
Suppliers of Paverpol fabric hardener, 0.1mm wire, small bobbins and knitted wire tubing. Crazy Wire is internet based, and doesn't have a shop. You are more than welcome to visit their warehouse but please call first to ensure it is convenient for someone to show you around.

Fasturn
3859 S Stage
Medford
Oregon 97501
Tel: 800-729-0280 / 541-772-8430
Email: sales@fasturn.net
www.fasturn.net
Suppliers of Fasturn fabric tube turning system, Fastube sewing foot, blue tubes and the large scale tube turner.

Craftynotions.com
Unit 2 Jessop Way
Newark
NG24 2ER
Tel: 01636 700862
Email: enquiries@craftynotions.com
www.craftynotions.com
Suppliers of banana yarn, environmentally friendly merino-cross wool tops and undyed nettle and hemp fibres. Visitors welcome by appointment or chance, please ring/email to avoid disappointment.

Lawrence Schiff Ribbons
Lawrence Schiff Silk Mills, Inc.
1385 Broadway, Suite 711
New York NY 10018
Phone: (212) 679-2185
Fax: (212) 696-4565
www.schiffribbons.com
Suppliers of earth-friendly biodegradable ribbons and hug snug rayon seam binding tape. (Hug snug seam binding tape is available from www.zipperstop.com who ship internationally.)

Lacis
Lacis Museum of Lace and Textiles
2982 Adeline St.
Berkeley, CA 94703
Tel: 510-843-7290
www.lacis.com
Suppliers of netting shuttles and netting needles.

Of The Earth
Kevin Graham
1226 South Angelo St.
Seattle WA 98108
kevin@custompaper.com
www.custompaper.com
Tel: 1.888.294.1526
Suppliers of Of The Earth eco-twist ribbon made with 50% recycled lotka fiber, 100% vegetable dyes, biodegradable, natural vegetable-dyed spools of hand twisted handmade paper ribbons.

Author's acknowledgements

In particular I would like to acknowledge the more than generous support given by Robin Smith (Texere Yarns) and Stuart Smethurst (Kemtex) for the inspiring fibres, dyes and other materials used in the sampling throughout the book. Thank you.

I would also like to thank Laura and Andy at The Crazy Wire Company, Mervyn Williams at Spunart, Kevin Graham from Of The Earth, and Mr Richard J. Schiff, president and CEO at Lawrence Schiff Ribbons. Thanks also to Sarah Lawrence at Craftynotions, all the staff at Fasturn and Ken at The Colorwheel Company.

To my partner Mick Pearce, thank you for the illustrations and diagrams, and not forgetting the cooking and the invaluable support, through yet another chaotic deadline.

Thank you also to Michael Wicks for the beautiful photography.

Health and safety

It is essential that you use all potentially hazardous materials and equipment responsibly, and that you make yourself aware of any health and safety issues. For example, make yourself aware of all known potential hazards from fumes, generated when burning any type of materials, and take the relevant precautions.

When using any type of chemical including solvents, glues, varnishes, bleach and dye powders read, and act on, the relevant health and safety guidelines for each product.

RSI (repetitive strain injury) is thought to be caused by repetitive movements, and can be a particular hazard to textile makers. If you think this is becoming a problem, seek professional advice. Consider wearing therapeutic craft gloves, if suitable.

Good posture, seating height and lighting are of paramount importance. If you sit for long hours, take regular breaks, and exercise back, neck and hand muscles in particular. Set a timer if all else fails to remind you to do this.

Although no chemical should be regarded as entirely hazard-free, fabric dyes for craft purposes, and associated chemicals, present a relatively low risk.

Note that this is so long as they are handled with proper precautions, and that the manufacturer's guidelines on health and safety are adhered to.

Clean and tidy habits should be maintained in both the use and storage of dyes and chemicals. Remember that bright colours and interesting bottles attract small children. Care should be taken when handling dyes and chemicals to avoid accidentally swallowing them.

Skin and eye contact should be avoided. If this occurs, wash the area for at least five minutes with cold, clean water. In the event of eye contact, seek qualified medical help as necessary, remembering to note the name of the chemical involved.

Safety guidelines

The following guidelines should be strictly adhered to when working with dyes:

- Always wear rubber gloves.

- A lab coat or full-fronted apron is recommended to protect against spillage.

- Safety spectacles with transparent sides (B&Q sell these) will provide eye protection.

- A simple filter-type mask (disposable) should be used when mixing dye powders. This is especially applicable if large quantities of dry powder are being used. Dust from hot- and cold-water reactive dyes is potentially harmful, and can cause sensitivities to build up in some people if breathed in. The reaction is similar to the effects of hay fever. Asthmatics should consider getting medical advice before proceeding at all.

- Avoid inhaling vapour from dye-pots. Adequate ventilation should dispose of any steam, but some chemicals, such as ammonia vapour, will irritate nasal passages.

- Always store dyes and auxiliary chemicals in properly labelled containers, out of reach of children. It is illegal to use ex-food containers such as lemonade bottles for such purposes.

- Use specially reserved equipment for dyeing. Do not use pots and pans for dyeing, and then use them for cooking the family meal later.

- If you are working at home, cover all work surfaces with newspapers to avoid contamination. Do not eat, drink or smoke in the dyeing area.

- Normal kitchen safety precautions regarding non-slippery floors and pans of boiling liquid should be observed.

The above rules are mainly common sense, and are intended to protect craft workers, rather than discourage them from proceeding at all.

Index